With Child

With Child

Mormon Women on Mothering

Edited by

Marni Asplund-Campbell

Signature Books
Salt Lake City

Cover illustration: David Adams, *Gabrael Zane Boogert*, 1992, pencil and photography

∞ *With Child* was printed on acid free paper and was composed, printed, and bound in the United States.

© 1998 Signature Books, Inc. Signature Books is a registered trademark of Signature Books, Inc.

02   01   2000   99   98   6   5   4   3   2   1

Library of Congress Cataloging-in-Publication Data
With child : Mormon women on mothering / edited by
    Marni Asplund-Campbell.
            p.   cm.
        ISBN 1-56085-112-0 (pbk.)
        1. Mormon women.   2. Motherhood—Religious
    aspects—Mormon Church.   3. Mormon Church—
    Membership.   4. Church of Jesus Christ of Latter-day
    Saints—Membership.   I. Asplund Campbell, Marni
    BX8641.T43W58   1998
    248.8'431'088283—dc21   98-15271
                                                CIP

Contents

Children

Loss

Editor's Introduction

Just a few weeks pregnant with my first baby, and not even two months married, I stood at a lobby pay phone in the Wilkinson Center at Brigham Young University in Provo, Utah, and called my parents to tell them the news. My father said, "Well, my dear, just look what you've begun."

Nearly a decade later, now I see almost as much significance in the context of that conversation as in the content. Knowing what I know now, I can hardly believe I dared to speak so eagerly the words that made public and real my motherhood. A generation earlier I probably would not have known, except by intuition, that I was pregnant, and I would have needed to visit a doctor to confirm the fact. But as a woman of the late twentieth century, I bought a test at Fred Meyer that told me, virtually in an instant, that I was, and with "99%" chemical accuracy. (My mother-in-law refused to believe it was true until I saw a real doctor.) A generation earlier, had I known of my condition, I scarcely would have dared tell anyone, let alone call my father, in a public place and share the news with such jolly confidence and biologically precise language. Looking back, I imagine that he must have been a little embarrassed by my enthusiasm.

My mother never knew during her pregnancies, as I did with mine, the gender of her babies before they were born, or their dimensions, weight, and the shapes of their hands and heads in utero. She never saw her cervix with the help of a mirror and speculum, or made a "birth plan," like I did, complete with instructions about episiotomies, enemas, and what she would wear during her delivery. I also knew, as so many generations of women before me could not, that I had a better-than-excellent chance of surviving the births of my children alive. I knew that my babies would most likely survive infancy. I knew all about the Rh factor, which must have been responsible for so many lost children, and gestational diabetes, which caused so many maternal deaths, and toxoplasmosis, and edema, and placenta previa, and the importance of folic acid in my diet.

I weep and cringe when I imagine my great-great-grandmother giving birth to triplets in a cold February cabin in New Harmony, Utah, losing all three of those tiny girls within a month of their births. I imagine her feeling, without Advil or codeine, the things I never knew until I had children—the pain of torn flesh, weakened muscles, and engorged breasts.

But most of all, I knew, as an expectant mother, as so very many of the women who lived before me, including my mother, did not, that my pregnancy came by choice. There was no question when I was going to be married that I could, and, some said, should practice contraception. I had an array of birth control options presented to me, all of which were available without too much expense, danger, or any social stigma. But at twenty-three I knew that I wanted nothing more than to be pregnant. I'd graduated from college, served a mission, and gotten married with quick efficiency. I knew that I was ready for the next frontier. So I said no thanks to the pill and was throwing up with morning nausea almost before my "honeymoon cystitis" ("Try just shaking hands for a while," the doctor at the health center said as he handed me my antibiotics) had cleared up. When I shared the news with friends and family, their reactions were more often, "Was that an accident?" and "Did you plan this?" than "Congratulations." While there may have been too much silence and secrecy about the mechanics of pregnancy and birth in earlier eras, there was also a tacit acceptance of the fact that, barring any physical impediments, married women had babies. But now I, and not biology, or fate, or the hand of God, was responsible for my pregnancy.

I have seen many, many friends agonize, in this completely new context, over the decision to have children. For with the choice comes a grim sort of accountability. We are not just empowered with the safety and hygiene of modern reproductive technology, we are also expected to know when we are truly ready to take on the job. And we impose harsh penalties on those we deem unfit. Once in a religion class at BYU, I sat silent as nearly the entire room of young LDS men and women expressed their feelings from disgust and even rage to embarrassment at the sight of a "battered old station wagon filled with too many kids in DI clothes." Such a sight was once the norm among Mormons—and now that it is clearly no longer a part of our culture, now that we ask those who would be parents to have comfortable incomes, homes, and college funds, we have not created a dialogue which explores the new choices we make, women make, when we decide to get pregnant.

I moved through my first pregnancy feeling that I lived in two distinct worlds. In one I studied Cicero and taught Dickens. I huddled over the space heater at night with my husband and read pages and pages of critical theory and Ibsen. In another dimension, literally underneath my skin, was this all-consuming universe within myself, so real I could close my eyes and see it growing. Nothing that I read or did in my public life explained to me the dark advent inside my body and soul. Nothing prepared me for the huge new emotions that left me speechless. I was desperate to read of other womens' pregnancies. I needed to know if this sense of being divided was normal. I wanted to hear someone else say it. And I wanted to know about labor. What would it feel like? I searched for writings and found very few that were not technical and dogmatic or vague and sentimental. So in my personal search for mother-texts, I began to make this book.

First, I wanted to find writings that addressed the new context of Mormon motherhood that I still find baffling. Joanna Brooks writes in "Alchemy" of a silent secret that kept the women in her family from bearing many children, as good women should, and her own very new plans for calling her children into the world. Eileen Gibbons Kump's beautiful story, "Bread and Milk," reminds us that pregnancy has always been a matter of public interest in Mormon culture, despite our occasional desire to bear it secretly. Allison Pingree's sermon, "Hearts Swelling 'Wide as Eternity,'" places the choice to become a parent in the context of Mormon scripture and theology, and Holly Welker's poem, "Where I'm From," reminds us that an artist's desire to have a child is so bewildering perhaps because it is entangled with so many other conflicting desires.

I also wanted to find writings that addressed the silence that surrounds so much of mothering experience. Tessa Santiago accuses her mother, in "Mother's Day," of failing to fill her in on the real pains of birth. Her mother responds that if she had, Tessa "would never have had a baby." While that may be true, Tessa concludes, there are some truths that, in all fairness, should be told. Pandora Brewer's earthy/ethereal journal entries speak some of the truth of the often unspoken ambivalence of pregnancy. Francine Bennion's "Death and Life" tells a powerful, draining story that is as much about the terror of silence as it is about the delivery and death of her first child. Margaret Young's description of birth in *Salvador* gives an uncommonly honest picture of the sounds, smells, and heat of birth. And Dian Saderup's story, "A Blessing of Duty," captures the silent joy, pain, and fear of an unplanned pregnancy.

Martha Sonntag Bradley's and Elizabeth Bradley's essays together present a stunning picture of silence overcome, of daughters and mothers sharing intimately the essential commonalities of mothering experience. The birth narratives of Stephanie Smith-Waterman, Arlene Burraston-White, and Julie Nichols provide what I wish I'd had when I was first pregnant: honest, first-hand accounts of birth that don't spare details of thoughtless fathers, enemas, and long labors.

As the manuscript grew, it took on different dimensions. While I hoped initially to focus on pregnancy and birth narratives, I found that many women could not talk about birth without talking about their subsequent lives with children. I began to search for manuscripts that would not only speak in the silence but that would create a new language for mothering experience. For many women, the language comes when they can find words to define time and causality in new ways, just as children force you to alter the rhythms of life. Karen Farb wrote her reflection on her experience of giving birth to and then giving away her daughter only after she came to realize, while raising her second child years later, how much that birth story was still filling her heart and mind, and demanding to be told. She gives new words to feelings of love and connection with a lost child and collapses the myth of past and present as separate realms. Dixie Lee Partridge's poems create delicate spots of time like shimmering prisms through which we see the refracted rays of hope and yearning for our children as they grow independent. Linda Sillitoe's "Charm for a Sick Child" and "For my sister, nearing armistice" introduce a mother-language that is a magical amalgamation of word and gesture. The heroine in Lara Candland's "Poetry" is lost for words in the world of her baby, and only in sleep discovers the slow poetry that is rising in her.

Some who have read this manuscript have asked me, "Why must it be so dark? Can't you just enjoy motherhood?" But great joy is never achieved without great pain, and without the words to say it, the joy cannot be complete. Julie Nichols writes in her story, "Pennyroyal, Cohosh, Rue," and her essay, "The Shadow Side of Mothering," of the darkness that is the twin part of the light of life. Her words remind us that we must all take care to communally nurture those who venture into parenthood and allow them to speak their sorrows. Heidi Hemming Smith's essay, "It Happens So Often," tells of two births and a death, and in drawing parallels between the events highlights the dark responsibility of privilege we enjoy in North America. Kim Barentsen's essay, "Spencer Roy Barentsen," gives words to a still-born child and creates deep beauty out of the deepest grief. Carol Bennion Quist, in her essay, "Red Roses for a Blue Lady," describes her life with a mentally disabled child and strips away the tender mythologies of mother-love, showing that often love means simply bearing the burden of physical care for another person, and sometimes handing that care over to someone else.

Jan Stucki writes in her essay, "What Nobody Told Me," that if we do not acknowledge that the language of mothering may also be the language of Eros, we may never see the full beauty of a child's body and a mother's body communicating in flesh. Susan Elizabeth Howe's poem, "Fighting With My Mother," and Dian Saderup's poem, "First Trimester," use images of combat between mother and child to highlight the resolution of love and affection. Finally, Louise Plummer's delightful "Instructions for My Funeral and Other Posthumous Thoughts" gives us the ultimate joy of a woman reflecting on her long and very happy life, showing that even in death, a wise woman finds humor and joy.

When I became pregnant for the first time, I felt—almost heard—a gentle entry of spirit into my body. When I tried to describe it to a friend, she laughed at my physiological ignorance. Of course the egg would not have been fertilized, let alone implanted, for several days after I claimed to know that I had conceived. Perhaps we have too many windows now. Perhaps we have lost a measure of the ephemeral mystery of spirit dwelling in soul to the shadowy ultrasound image. For I know that I knew, in the very moment, that my husband and I had created a life.

I see through a window my Eliza, staring though glass that is bubbled with rain. She has giant gaps in her teeth, and holes in the knees of her linty tights. She is tapping hello with her fingertips, through the shop window, and my car windshield, hello and see my new haircut, hello, and come to get me now. Hello and I love you more than you love me.

Conception

Alchemy

Joanna Brooks

THIS STORY BEGINS, RIGHTLY, in my mother's house. Married at nineteen, she was in her third year at Brigham Young University, auburn hair and ivory skin, and weighing 106 pounds on her wedding day. *106 pounds*, she tells me.

My father crossed the river bed to join her. Doing so, he moved precious miles outward from Los Angeles's urban center, leaving his less noble Okie neighborhood, the meat-packing places and factories, the house where his mother, alone, raised her four sons (and prized roses) on double-shift salaries and biscuits, the recipe for which was so automatic that she never thought to write it down. It's lost to us now.

Together, as handsome couples did in those days, my father and mother made steady, blessed progress, getting ever more suburban. They bought a first house on two salaries. Too soon it seemed too small for their boundless enterprise, and their move to the second house, I figure, was precipitated by me—or by the hope of me.

Which hope I held off for some time, testing their faith in the promises and portents. It took doctors, lawyers, and bishops—prescription bottles, preliminary adoption counseling, and priesthood blessings—to coax the elements into place and the natural into action.

I was their first, as my mother was her mother's first, and only. My grandmother, in fact, gave her mother the Dorton family's only granddaughter. The four Dorton girls produced only two children. This is rare in a Utah family. There are reasons for this—some cruel apocrypha I have heard, and much more I haven't. Most of my Dorton great-aunts are dead now, the causes only whispered. Their photos curl, perpetually drying, from the black-paper family albums into which they are pasted.

I was fourteen when I got my patriarchal blessing. I was a miraculous fourteen, with a huge mind and extensive sensitivity, of which my generously sized A-cup took no notice. Back then, I may have matched my mother's legendary *106 pounds*.

I fasted before my blessing, and it was lovely, and of all that was said one bit stuck out. In the most reliable part of the blessing, the part about marriage and family, the patriarch said something about me being a "Mother in Israel" and teaching the children that would be "placed" in my "home."

"Mother in Israel," of course, being the conciliatory phrase they use to comfort the childless women in the church. And the ambiguity of "placed"—sounding too close to "Indian Placement Program," sounding distinctly like *adoption*. Why not "You will bear"? Or even "You will have"?

I don't know if the patriarch realized what kind of fear he seeded in me, how these small phrases took root in my head. Already I was a smart girl. Already my sister MIA Maids Juli and Shayne seemed much more lush and swollen. Already I was fourteen and tapping the calendar, waiting, nothing moving yet. I imagined my ovaries—almond-sized, they say?—dry-roasted inside of me. Husks, just husks.

When I left for BYU, everyone teased me about going just for my "MRS" degree. Me, of all people, with a scholarship and all. No joke: I spent freshman orientation in horror, utterly panicked by the huge hordes of bright boys with wheat-colored hair and lip-glossed girls, and wondering how was I ever going to find a husband?

When I was twenty, the doctor diagnosed me with polycystic ovaries. "Which means?" I asked. "You don't ovulate," she said.

Seminary taught me how to read the signs, how to see the secret meanings. I have pondered all these things in my heart.

Writing this, I am just turned twenty-four, still single, and six years out of the house. I have a small, bright apartment in Los Angeles—lots of books, big windows, white walls, bright colors, wood floors. I clean the house carefully and often. I am grateful for this place; I have worked hard to establish it.

Sometimes my parents wonder why I stay shut up in it with so many books. They love me. "Don't miss out on Prince Charming," they say.

"If he's Prince Charming, he'll wait around until I've passed my doctoral exams," I say, and I mostly believe it. My exams are seven weeks away.

When my mother presses me on the subject, I remind her that I have enlisted four sperm donors, just in case. One is my boxing coach, one is a hiking guide in southern Utah, one is a wanderlust poet-type and soon to be doctor, and one is a fellow graduate student in literature, a brilliant, handsome man. The plan goes like this: they donate, they get lost, I raise the kid with my best friend Karen and assorted other women friends of all ages on a refuge ranch we call "The Tofu Farm." The men show up on special days and weekends, bearing gifts, taking the kids out on high-adventure sports outings, with the provision that if it's rock climbing or gun shooting, I get to come along for fun. Then the men impart terse but tender bits of wisdom, and get lost again. They've all endorsed the plan. These four, they're good stock, I reassure her. She is not reassured.

Sometimes, yes, I resent the way she recommends "the bigger picture" to me—how the words "husband" and "babies" operate for her, and thus for me, as keys to a "wider world." I resist the way her life wraps around mine, contextualizes mine. To her I have not yet "arrived," and will not until I am carried over that threshold or become someone else's doorway.

I am, however, arriving at this conclusion: whatever thresholds I cross or doorways I erect will stand within her world, not take me out of it. I am woman and adult enough to know that I am and always will be of my mother's house, whoever comes along. I honor the stories already written for me; I occupy them proudly and in their shelter write new ones.

In this version, however, nothing's hung up over help-on-the-way, be it keys or alchemy. I say—moving into bigger rooms, now; widening hard won spaces; calling stars into place, countless ones, perhaps.

Morning Song

Marion Bishop

IT HAPPENED AGAIN LAST NIGHT: I gave birth to a tiny baby
girl in my sleep. She was light and bright and beautiful and I cradled her
in my arms and smoothed the thin, blonde hair over the soft spot on
her head. When she became hungry, I nursed her from my swollen
breast. Sometime near dawn her baby noises woke me and I stumbled
through the dark into the bathroom. I turned on lights, drank water,
and sat on the edge of the tub holding my face in my hands. I am
twenty-seven years old. I have never been pregnant or given birth to a
child.

But all around me, friends are having babies. I listen to colleagues
and college roommates discuss breast-pumps and Pampers; I go to baby
showers and send flowers to celebrate new births. I listen as friends,
married and not, confide about family planning and strategically chart
the births of their children against grids of career goals and the number
of child-bearing years they have left. I am quiet in an awkward way during these conversations and don't know what to say when well-meaning people, knowing that my husband and I want a family, ask when we
will have our first child. I swallow tears at the back of my throat and
keep silent the secret that I cannot yet have a baby.

But the dreams keep coming: I am seven months pregnant and another woman, tall and lean with a basketball belly, comes to me and
asks, please, can I carry her baby alongside mine. I respond a firm no,
but somehow the dream fetus is given to me and it wrestles in my womb
next to my own. This dual pregnancy doesn't work: my water breaks
and I give birth prematurely to twins. They both die.

In my waking hours I have spent the last five years recovering from
an eating disorder. For the first twenty-two years of my life, I lived in a
body whose soul belonged to someone else with a man's voice and pen-

chant for work, production, and perfection. At his hands I became a perfect Sylvia-Plath-over-achiever: an all-American good-girl whose starve-binge cycle left her voiceless. I made straight A's, ran five miles a day, and rocked myself to sleep at night with chocolate and promises of starving. I rattled and shook inside myself until the false image broke. From its death came the children of my baby-dreams.

Often in these dreams I am rescuing, saving babies. One thirteen-month-old girl has been left in a car seat her whole life: strapped in on the passenger side of an ugly four-door sedan. She is starving and covered with her own feces and sweat and tears. I unbuckle the car seat and take her soiled, innocent body in my arms. We enter a dark, unfamiliar house where I bathe her, feed her, love her. I turn on lights and promise to keep her from the car seat.

In my professional life, I teach a class at Chicago's Roosevelt University to adults who have returned to school. Most have overcome tremendous personal and professional obstacles to bring themselves back to school at middle age. We read together Toni Morrison's *Beloved* and watch as Sethe, Paul D., and Denver confront the pain of their pasts and make lives for themselves they can own. We rock and mourn and churn with the book, learning from it and one another.

The worst dream came last week: I have lived through ten hours of natural childbirth—I have needed to own my womanness and my ability to bear a child in a way that drug-quieted labor would not allow. I am exhausted but my baby is born. The hospital is white and sterile and stainless steel. The men in the room do not have faces, only huge mouths and deep voices behind tightly-tied surgical masks. I reach for my baby and am rebuked. Loud, monosyllabic words frame what is wrong with her: head too long, weighs too much, come too soon. I snatch my baby from their large, cold hands, wrap us both in one clean, white sheet, and flee the hospital on stumbling, blood-stained legs.

I have a friend who had an abortion in the days before *Roe v. Wade*. At eighteen and already struggling to raise a pre-school-age son on her own when she discovered she was pregnant again, she felt she only had two options. The women's rights organization, that arranged for the abortion and stayed with her while it was performed on a kitchen table in a posh New York City suburb, feared detection by the authorities and urged her not to go to an emergency room, no matter how bad her hemorrhaging became. She took the bus home after the procedure and spent a week in bed recovering from the flu. She is clear with anyone who asks that abortion saved her life: her other option was suicide.

When I was four years old, my parents gave me a doll for Christmas that I named Baby Marion. By Valentine's Day I had already given her a haircut with my safety scissors and there were marks on her plastic legs and face where a neighborhood boy had drawn on her with a crayon. But I loved her deeply and would respond with tight hugs and outpourings of four-year-old affection every time she rolled on her stomach and said, "Maaa, Maaa."

I hear this child doll crying today and know I must respond. I call my parents and ask them to pull Baby Marion from the dark, crowded cedar closet where she has lived for the last twenty years. The UPS man brings her a few days later. I touch her jagged hair and smooth my fingers over her stained face. I hold her tightly to me, and when I am ready to let go, I place her on my desk next to a black-and-white photograph of me taken when I was two and a half years old.

All around me my friends are having babies. In my quiet, pre-dawn moments, I sit in the bathroom gathering courage to begin living my baby's dream. When the sun comes up, I leave the bathroom and find myself curled in my great-grandmother's rocking chair, acknowledging the pain of having a labor and delivery story that is so difficult to tell, a body whose stretchmarks and full breasts only I can see, and a baby I can't introduce to friends but who cries and wakes me in the night. I draw my knees to my chest, wrap my arms tightly around myself, and look out on Chicago's cool, grey morning. I sing songs to my infant, coo softly to her, and accept the awkward, tender recognition that in her survival comes my own.

Hearts Swelling "Wide as Eternity"
A Talk for Mother's Day

Allison Pingree

I APPRECIATE THE CHANCE TO speak today, both as part of our sacrament service and on this day when we focus on motherhood. I have spent several weeks pondering this talk, and I pray that my words may be expressed, and received, through the help of the Lord's spirit.

I have wondered, for the past several years, why we devote a worship service as central as sacrament meeting to Mother's Day. That is, why dedicate our principal meeting to a characteristic that is, in a technical sense, not a matter of spirituality but of biology? To a role that not all of us in the congregation can or do share in—either currently, or ever?

As I ponder these questions, I am haunted by the voice of a friend who, with her husband, has tried for many years to become a mother and has been physically unable. For her, Mother's Day is excruciating because it only reminds her, in a service where she hopes for religious communion, of what she lacks. Many mothers I know are similarly uncomfortable with such meetings because their idealizations often create more depression than celebration. I remember that, as I was growing up, my own mother, after hearing talks putting mothers on pedestals, often came home discouraged because of how aware she was that she wasn't perfect. While these questions and concerns continue to trouble me, I nonetheless do not want to brush motherhood or parenthood aside altogether, because focusing on it gives us the opportunity to learn some particular lessons about becoming like Christ and, in an obvious extension, like our Heavenly Parents. So today I would like to use parenthood as a metaphor; doing so will, I hope,

9

make us understand our literal parents (and our parenting, for those who are parents now) better, but also will help us look towards Christ as our ultimate model.

Since I am not a biological parent, the best way for me to compare parenthood and being Christ-like is to probe my feelings—both my anticipated joys and fears—about the prospect of becoming one. In that spirit I would like to share a few of those impressions with you, drawing analogies to Christ and our heavenly parents. I realize that many of you may not share my feelings regarding parenthood; nonetheless, I believe that the qualities I describe will help us explore the challenges involved in becoming like Christ.

One aspect of parenthood that seems especially daunting to me is having responsibility for a living, breathing person—being involved in a project with the most real and important of consequences. I have felt this anxiety before. When at age fifteen and a half I was first learning to drive, my father took me out, early one Sunday morning, in our blue Chevrolet station wagon to practice on a quiet side street in our neighborhood. I distinctly remember that as I first pushed the gas pedal and gripped the wheel, I thought of all the possible lives that would be in my hands over the years as I drove—friends, family, children—and how easily those lives could be ruined with one wrong turn. Although I was crawling along at only five miles an hour or so, these images flooded me with such an overwhelming sense of responsibility that tears spilled down my cheeks. As I contemplate parenting, I feel once again to be behind that wheel, facing the very sobering and very adult burden of caring for human life.

Part of the reason that responsibility seems so heavy is its necessary involvement in both physical and emotional pain. I have heard many stories of excruciating labors and deliveries, and know how, especially in previous generations, a woman bearing a child edges very close to death. I also see all around me the physical, financial, and emotional labor exerted by both mothers and fathers in raising those children once they are born.

Christ, of course, is the one who best understands and experiences the burdens of responsibility, as he atoned for our sins: "For behold, I, God, have suffered these things for all, that they might not suffer if they would repent" (D&C 19:16). Moreover, Christ descended below all things to feel our pain with us, as King Alma described in Alma 7:11-12:

> And he shall go forth, suffering pains and afflictions and temptations of every kind; and this that the word might be fulfilled which saith he will take upon him the pains and sicknesses of his people. And he will take upon him death, that he may loose the bands of death which bind his people; and he will take upon him their infirmities, that his bowels may be filled with mercy, according to the flesh, that he may know according to the flesh how to succor his people according to their infirmities.

What seems crucial here is that Christ is willing to feel things with us, to experience our pains and vulnerabilities so that we, moved to know that someone has been there and thus understands us and still loves us, are moved to turn to him for forgiveness and solace. Not only am I concerned by parenthood's burdens of responsibility, but also by knowing how much to give, wondering how to keep the boundaries of myself stable enough so as to have something to offer, yet flexible enough to do so. In considering this dialectic, I have been both heartened and chastened by Scott Peck's definition of love in *The Road Less Travelled* as "the will to extend one's self for one's own or another's spiritual growth" (81). Peck emphasizes that to truly love, we must have a self to extend, and that love is easily confused with control or dependence. He relates a story of a man who was debilitated by a mother who "loved him so much" that she drove him to school all the way through high school, "protecting" him from taking the bus on his own (82). As Peck later concludes,

> Love is not simply giving; it is judicious giving and judicious withholding as well. ... The word "judicious" means requiring judgment, and judgment requires more than instinct; it requires thoughtful and often painful decision-making (111).

> [N]ot giving at the right time [is] more compassionate than giving at the wrong time, and ... fostering independence [is] more loving than taking care of people who could otherwise take care of themselves (113).

It seems to me that Christ is able to strike the perfect balance in the dilemma of selfhood and giving, because he is at once utterly selfless yet utterly clear on his mission, his personal power, and our individual needs.

Toni Morrison affirms the importance of a sense of self as she describes how parenting forced her to be distinctly who she was and no one else:

> [Becoming a mother] was the most liberating thing that ever happened to me. ... Liberating because the children's demands on me were things that nobody else asked me to do. To be a good manager. To have a sense of humor. To deliver something that somebody could use. And they were not interested in all the things that other people were interested in, like what I was wearing or if I were sensual. I could not only be me—whatever that was—but somebody actually needed me to be that (quoted in Bill Moyers, *A World of Ideas III*).

As Christians, too, we are needed for ourselves, for what we can offer as individual gifts. As Paul tells us, all parts are necessary to the body of the Christian community—we are all both utterly distinct and symbolically united:

> For by one Spirit are we all baptized into one body, whether we be Jews or Gentiles, whether we be bond or free; and have been all made to drink into one Spirit. For the body is not one member, but many. ... If the whole body were an eye, where were the hearing?
>
> If the whole were hearing, where were the smelling? But now hath God set the members every one of them in the body, as it hath pleased him. ... That there should be no schism in the body; but that the members should have the same care one for another. And whether one member suffer, all the members suffer with it; or one member be honoured, all the members rejoice with it. Now ye are the body of Christ, and members in particular (1 Cor. 12:13, 14, 17-18, 25-27).

A final dilemma that parenting presents to me is its demand for a deep emotional investment in a person whose actions I cannot control, and who may very well reject or hurt me. Indeed, I have observed my parents' pain and confusion as I have made choices contradicting their own desires and ideals, and have been moved by their continued efforts to connect with me despite these conflicts.

Christ, of course, epitomizes this capacity for empathy. For instance, although he knew of his ability to raise Lazarus from death, he "groaned in the spirit" and was "troubled," as Lazarus's family grieved. Few passages of scripture convey so briefly yet so powerfully Christ's willingness to share the pain of those who suffer as the subsequent simple verse, "Jesus wept" (John 11:33, 35). Indeed, Christ's mission enacts the incalculable and terrifying risk of caring for, and feeling with, those who may at any time betray that bond.

Our Heavenly Father is equally committed to the risk of empathic involvement. This willingness is illustrated in a particularly moving manner when, in the Book of Moses in the Pearl of Great Price, Enoch receives a vision of the world to come—of Christ, Satan, angels, heavens, and all the inhabitants of earth—and then notices something astonishing:

> And it came to pass that the God of heaven looked upon the residue of the people, and he wept; and Enoch bore record of it, saying: How is it that the heavens weep, and shed forth their tears as the rain upon the mountains? And Enoch said unto the Lord: How is it that thou canst weep, seeing thou art holy, and from all eternity to all eternity? And were it possible that man could number the particles of the earth, yea, millions of earths like this, it would be a beginning to the number of thy creations; and thy curtains are stretched out still; and yet thou art there, and thy bosom is there; and also thou art just; thou art merciful and kind forever; And thou hast taken Zion to thine own bosom, from all thy creations, and from all eternity to all eternity; and naught but peace, justice, and truth is the habitation of thy throne; and mercy shall go before thy face and have no end; how is it thou canst weep?
>
> The Lord said unto Enoch: Behold these thy brethren; they are the workmanship of mine own hands, and I gave unto them their knowledge, in the day I created them; and in the Garden of Eden, gave I unto man his agency; And unto thy brethren have I said, and also given commandment, that they should love one another, and that they should choose me, their Father; but behold, they are without affection, and they hate their own blood. ... and misery shall be their doom; and the whole heavens shall weep over them, even all the workmanship of mine hands; wherefore should *not* the heavens

weep, seeing these shall suffer? (Moses 7:28-33, 37; emphasis added)

Here Enoch is privileged with a glimpse into God's heart, into the emotional anguish that even he, in his majesty and wisdom, feels for his children. Strikingly, God's empathy and compassion affects Enoch so deeply that he, too, is moved to tears; as he sees the "wickedness" and "misery" of the "children of men," Enoch "wept and stretched forth his arms, and his heart swelled wide as eternity; and his bowels yearned; and all eternity shook" (v. 41).

This scene poses, I think, a model for us all—a model of the demands of being a Christian, of being willing and able to experience others' pain, and thus help to heal them. As Alma tells us in Mosiah 18:8-10, we are to "bear one another's burdens, that they may be light; yea, and are willing to mourn with those that mourn; yea, and comfort those that stand in need of comfort."

In conclusion, on this day, even as flowers are given to women only, and even as the Primary children sing songs about literal mothers, it is my prayer that we will extend the meanings of motherhood—and of *parenthood*—beyond biology, to a focus on Christ, and towards our spiritual parents. I believe that as we muster the courage to be responsible to each other, as we respect ourselves as distinct members of the body of Christ with valuable contributions to make, as we suffer and rejoice with our brothers and sisters, as we weep and "stretch forth our arms"—that our hearts, like Enoch's, will "swell wide as eternity." For indeed eternity is unfolding now, as we nurture, minister to, and give life to all those around us.

Deep in My Trunk

Julie Turley

I BRING ONE OF THOSE TOSSAWAY cameras to the wedding and use all fifteen shots on the bride coming up the aisle. Her hairstyle is the most magnificent thing about the wedding and this is what I want to capture. It is a complex sentence with many rooms, all false. The blonde cupola on top holds a tiara, which is fraught with rhinestones—a pageant gift the bride won in Utah Valley at sixteen.

The bride is thirty-two and pregnant. We find this out in the basement bathroom of the Salt Lake Arts Center where the reception is. The test stick turns pink, and before the dancing, she takes off her hair, which she hands to me for the box, which is aqua, the color of feminine hygiene. Now my friend looks like Mia Farrow when she was Mrs. Sinatra. I put the wig and the stick in the box and run it out to my car which is parked across the street at the mall. My friend, being Mormon, was married as close to the temple as she could get, in the Lion House, next to the Beehive House.

I was married once and tried to get pregnant all the way through it. Then I broke it off, had everything ripped out, cleaned out. They found something troubling, and I didn't want to take any chances.

Back inside, I lean into the basement bathroom mirror where other female guests mill before the band starts and clean up my lipstick. It is a deep ruddy red autumn stick that I drop in my bra as I tear up the stairs.

The band launches into something from *The Lion King* and I want to be there for the first dance. My friend, the bride, takes the elbow of her new husband—not the father of this child who accompanies them across the floor, we both know. This new husband, heartbreakingly enough, is a virgin, and runs his free hand over his hair, and then the other over the bride's. They begin to foxtrot, and, before the song ends, foxtrot to the table of honor and everyone cracks up.

At the buffet I load up on prawns and miniature rice cakes with nicoise-style olives. It is a heady, eclectic buffet, and I raise my strawberry frappe punch in a tribute to the table of honor. They raise theirs back, and then, predictably enough, the bride bends her sleek head into a beaded bridal bag. I meet her in the bathroom and give her my lipstick for a touch up.

"What did you do with the stick?" she asks.

"I kept it," I say.

We look in the mirror at each other. Someone has been smoking in here, and I mist the room with perfume—a cheap copy of Joy. My hair has been swept up into a simple chignon, and my dress has been so expertly cut that I am undetectable when I sweep into a room.

I am all about myself, nothing else.

Thinking of Me

Julie Turley

MY HUSBAND'S COUSIN HAD TO give the baby she had just adopted back after she had already named it. The court order made me laugh bitterly, and I choked on the Grape Nuts and soy milk I eat every night like a child. The man who contested the adoption was the father—a septaugenarian from West Covina, California. He took the baby and stuck it in one of those plastic walkers.

A trashed-out polaroid of this lands in my husband's cousin's post office box, and she brings it over and throws it on our trashed-out couch.

I finish my cereal and almost sit on it, the photograph. The cousin plops down beside me. If I weren't Mormon, I would have a cigarette, I am so satisfied from dinner, that humble bowl. I bring my fingers to my mouth and inhale, faking it.

I have not told a lie in months. Except now I tell the cousin that she would have made an excellent mother, and that if I had seven babies, I would give her half. At my advanced age—thirty-three—I would need a little help.

We laugh together, and not one hour later, I am foraging through my cupboards for more food. But there is nothing, only powdered milk, powdered eggs, baby red lentils—dry—and a magnificent fruit cake still boxed.

We have no baby. One has not been sent to us, boxed or otherwise.

My grandmother calls and hangs up when I answer. She thinks I am keeping a good old-fashioned pregnancy from her on purpose.

Something is wrong with us here. Our bed is on wooden stilts. The skirt of our couch drags the surface of our battered parquet floors. We are in New York City, and our neighbor above us throws herself onto the floor like a bomb.

"Nothing sticks," the weatherman says, thinking of me. My husband's face drifts. He is thinking of his cousin and the first baby she had named Hope who she lost in the ninth month before she could slam herself against the wall of her Westchester nursery and push it out of herself. The family buried it under the huge storm that swept us the winter of 1996.

In West Covina the seventy-year-old father drags the walker across the carpet. His baby's legs dangle helplessly underneath.

Far away, in Utah, is where all babies are so effortlessly grown, attaching themselves to uterine walls like the snow on our fire escape that lengthens into ice.

Where I'm From

Holly Welker

As if devotion to beauty
made the emptiness meaningful,
like women embroidering the forbidden stitch
on the garments of Chinese emperors,
women squinting and concentrating until they went blind.
I thought if I looked at enough worlds
I'd find one I wanted to be a citizen of
and now I've chosen by default
to be a stranger where I've always lived.
And I thought too that despite voyages
to continents my parents never saw,
I was sheltered, naive, even almost pure;
in bewildering moments I realize it *hurts*
to discover I'm right, and I find myself
stroking my lover's face,
wishing he were my son.

A Delicate Condition

A Hope Invisible

Pandora Brewer

TODAY IS FRIDAY. ON WEDNESDAY of this week I heard the first proof positive that Mark and I are going to have a baby. A faint, fast heartbeat that seemed related more to the static of the Doppler device than the human race. Yet, as the volume ebbed and jerked with his movement, the reality of this five-inch person assuaged four months of wonder, fear, and disbelief. I haven't written in over half a year. I spent the end of the summer and the early fall trying to define some sort of future for myself. I was promoted quickly through Crate and Barrel, allowing myself to be groomed for upper management. I would alternately reach for retail power only to pull back and contemplate education and literary greatness. The want for a baby vacillated with equal intensity. Mark wanted to wait, but was softening. I was aching to be pregnant (ignorant fool that I was) but attempting to talk myself into establishing some order in my personal life first. I felt this urgency because I imagined that it would take months to get pregnant. I had heard so many horror stories about infertility and had always felt this nagging guilt about waiting so long. I thought that one had to prepare the ground like planting a crop, or maybe just practice a while. We were hardly teenagers in someone's back seat. Mark snorted at my physiological naivete, either the connection was made or it wasn't, age and target practice had little to do with it. We became a tad lax on the condom use, anyway. The first month we even approximated ovulation, my notions of agriculture were trashed and I felt a lot like a teenager after all.

I knew almost immediately that I was pregnant. The body changes were sudden and dramatic. The doctor called to confirm the test right in the middle of my six-month review at work, almost at the moment that I was being guaranteed a management position the next month.

My reaction surprised me. After at least five years of wistfully wishing and dreaming and drooling over babies, I felt an unexplainable darkness. I envisioned myself on a time-line and for the first time sensed with palpable clarity my own mortality.

This pregnancy has been a strange, lonely experience. Even as I sit here, a pillow propped behind my curving back and my stomach bulging around the edge of the table, there is an unreality about this transition that is unnerving. I can feel the constant creeping and stretching of this new life. I can see the taut skin on my abdomen quiver like a drum when it kicks. Every time I think that surely this stomach can get no bigger, it does. Yet when I hold babies or stare at them or wonder about them, there is a gap in my understanding that my imagination tries vainly to fill. I still can't fathom how this unseen movement is going to emerge somehow as my baby, my child. I know how to care for children, but have always given them back, most of the time gladly. I can give love but have never sensed utter dependency from another human being. It is difficult for me to imagine how something can be part of me and yet separate only to become separate but still connected. I want this baby to be a true, happy child. Greta Garbo died last week with an epitaph, *I want to be alone.* I sit here beating with two lives and I want to scream, *Don't leave me alone.* But alone I must write. And alone this baby will decide whether or not he will be true or happy.

And amid all these swirling worries, I am intolerably impatient. Ten months is a lifetime. I feel that I have created a generation of mental babies in the time it has taken to produce one physical one. I have fourteen weeks left, not including the probable two-week, first-baby tease. What a contrast the second pregnancy must be to the first. The little personality may be different, but the calmness of knowing at least generally what to expect must be comforting. The wait would have a tested limit, the finale would be a remembered anticipation.

Give or take a week or two, I am about one month away from giving birth. It could happen anytime I suppose, although in spite of my enormous size, none of the pre-labor signs have taken place. I know that the baby hasn't engaged in my pelvis yet because I still have feet in my lungs. Either that or he is thirty inches long, which I doubt. The past month has been good. My spirits are up and amazingly my energy level is higher than at any point in the pregnancy. I feel more confident about the reality of being a mother; I feel hopeful in my ability to be productive amidst the transition.

I have twelve more days until my due date, whatever that means. My stomach is my center. My brain, my heart, and self have become a squirming, swelling planet. I feel completely disassociated from any sense of humanness. I am merely a container, a reservoir, a fixture that is controlled by forces completely arbitrary. I am one of those demi-goddesses who is raped by Zeus in the form of raindrops or something and is never quite sure what has happened. This conception has a father but the result is still as mystifying. Who is this creature who has grown tyrannical in its power? I am ruled by an object larger than anything else in my body. Perhaps it has swallowed all of my organs to make room for itself. Perhaps I feel so tired and empty because there is nothing left inside for me to exist. It may be the baby's heart that beats for both of us. I wonder if I will wither and die like a shed skin when this new being chooses its freedom. I don't remember what it is like to be small and light and one. Ironically, since sharing my body, I have never been so alone or isolated. I am connected to a process over which I have no control. I am moved upon by the gods and stand witness to a miracle that can never be truly shared. With my vision I am separate; I feel truth that has no language, a hope invisible.

I still cannot grasp the reality of my situation. I have read and browsed and stared at pictures, trying to attach an infant's figure to the slow rolling lumps in my abdomen, but I cannot. I look at children in the street and think, I'm not ready, or I can be a good mother, or Help. My ambivalence is moody and I cry a lot. Mark attempts strength and won't discuss his feelings in order to save me anxiety. He has told me this. He doesn't understand that his stoic, almost cold demeanor only heightens my barriers. I see myself as ill or bizarre or weak because only I wonder if I truly want this baby. Only I worry about a marriage plagued with doubt. Only I dream of a cabin and a computer far away from anyone or anywhere. Mark pats my head gently and coos words of comfort while impassively going about life as if he were the last fiber of rationality in our relationship. I am banging, foaming waves, and he is as placid as a pond. Only his eyes betray repressed tension. He pushes back fear like his foot smashing garbage farther down in the can, making room for more. How much can he contain? I can hold the secrets of life in my womb, I can hold the most ancient of sorrows and pain. Can he understand or assimilate or even be aware of any of this? I wish he would talk to me. I wish I were not the single fragile half that I am perceived to be. I wish he would let me prove myself strong enough to listen to his private insanity. I wish he would treat me like his companion and lover and not the hormone-wracked vessel of his child. I could then sense my own identity amid this symbiotic waiting. I could know that somewhere in my body is a part that has not been swallowed, a shred that is still glowing with an intensity undimmed by fatigue and hysteria and anger. A thin shining self that is as clear and lucid as the muse it protects. Quietly, behind the baby, behind my endless complaints, part of me waits for another birth. My voice lies ready to speak.

First Trimester

Dian Saderup

Less than a speck and then a tadpole, now
you are a tiny alligator in
size—two inches of mostly head. Allow
me this: your unreality distend-
ing so slightly my waist, I cannot feel
you as you; you are a tiredness to
bonescore, a sickness refusing repeal.
In the pregnant sleepless hours of night, true
terror blooms big in me—this my body
taken hostage by your all-consuming
innocence. Such benign voracity
strangely tokens death, my life entombing
yours, yours mine.
          But grow. Always grow. Growing—
at last—out of me, this season's sowing
patiently perfected.

A Blessing of Duty

Dian Saderup

CAROLYN LAID THE BABY IN the crib, quickly putting a pacifier in his mouth. The crib sheet, she noticed, was sticky where Jennie had been playing earlier and dribbled orange juice from one of the baby's bottles. She must remember to wash it. The baby was irritable tonight. She'd kept him up purposely till after 10 hoping he would sleep through the night. Jennie, Becky, and Kevin were already bedded down. Jeff was still over at school practicing for the state basketball tournament, and Susan was spending the night with a girlfriend. Carolyn felt a quick twinge of remorse for having let her go on a school night. She switched off the light in the yellow nursery and closed the door to the baby's tired fussing. The pacifier had already fallen from his mouth.

Dr. Neilson wouldn't be able to see her until Friday.

Walking down the hall, she checked to make sure the night-light was on in the girls' room. In just the last few weeks Jennie had become terrified of the dark. Carolyn and Paul were wakened nearly every night by her screams. Two days ago Paul had installed a night-light next to the girls' trundle bed. It seemed to help. Carolyn hoped it would work tonight. She was tired tonight.

Dr. Neilson's nurse had a pleasant voice over the phone: "How 'bout 11:45, Mrs. Mecham? ... Good. We'll see you then." The test would be quick and simple.

The front door opened. That would be Jeff or maybe Paul if high council meeting had let out on time. She padded down the hallway.

"Hi, Mom."

"How was practice?"

"It's going good. We can take state this year. We're playing Orem in two days. If we win we're in the finals."

"Good, Son. I'm sure you'll win."

"Yeah, Orem'll be no sweat. Is Dad home?"

"No, he's still at council meeting."

"Oh yeah, I forgot." He turned and walked through the living room into the kitchen. He was taller than Paul now. Dr. Neilson had delivered Jeff. "Do we have any of that cake left, Mom?" he called and she could hear him rifling through cupboards.

"Shh ... Jeff," she whispered loudly, following him into the kitchen. "You'll wake the children. No, the cake is gone. Kevin and Becky split the last piece watching *Happy Days*. I didn't know you liked marble cake, Jeff. Last time I made it you told me you were tired of marble cake."

"I know but I'm starving."

"Have a glass of milk."

He went to the fridge and pulled out a carton of milk. As he poured it, he splashed milk on the formica counter top and linoleum floor. "Be careful, Jeff. I just waxed the floor today."

"Sorry." He guzzled the milk, spilling it down his chin and basketball jersey. "Night, Mom." He walked from the kitchen.

"Night, Son." She watched him, then, weary, bent to wipe the milk from the floor. Jeff would be eighteen next month, graduating from school in six. Dr. Neilson would smile when he said, "Carolyn, you're pregnant again." Gladys Mitchell's son had been killed in a car accident up Millcreek Canyon two days before his eighteenth birthday. He'd been drinking. Jeff went to priesthood with Paul every Sunday and blessed the sacrament in the afternoon. Carolyn didn't think that Jeff drank, but lots of mothers didn't know what their sons were doing. Beth Bower's son Mike, a friend of Jeff's and active in the ward, had been arrested not long ago on a drug charge. But Jeff was a good boy. He paid his tithing and went to church and last week he had conducted family home evening. Sometimes Carolyn wondered if Jeff parked with the girls he dated. She didn't want to be pregnant again. She was thirty-nine years old.

A pile of freshly laundered clothes was heaped on the table, whites, the last batch of the day. She sat down heavily on one of the vinyl kitchen chairs, pressing her face hard into the clothes. The soft cotton of a pair of Paul's garments felt clean and comfortable against her face.

She turned her head to breathe. The zipper in the garment bit her ear. She and Paul hadn't been to the temple in over a month. Carolyn often slept during parts of the ceremony, and, although she didn't understand much of the symbolism involved, she usually came home from a session refreshed and determined to be a better mother, make her home more a house of God, like the temple. President David O. McKay had said that a good Mormon home was like the celestial kingdom. Paul once told her that gods never stopped having children, that was what was meant by Eternal Life. He would be happy if she were pregnant. This week she needed to go to the temple.

The whites smelled of fabric softener. Every day she did at least six batches of laundry. She lifted her face from the clothes and picked Paul's garments from the pile. Then she folded Jeff's t-shirts and boxer shorts and stacked them separately and soon the table was lined with neat piles of panties, socks, undershirts, slips.

She gripped the edges of the vinyl chair and arched her back. Her lower back ached every night now. David was eight months old and big for his age. It strained her back to lift him. When she'd been pregnant with him, after the fifth month her back had ached constantly. During the last three weeks of the pregnancy, the pain became so severe that she'd had to stay in bed the entire time. Dr. Neilson had prescribed a pill for pain and told her that backache was quite common among expectant mothers, especially in women nearing their forties.

She looked at the wooden plaque which hung above the kitchen door. It read Choose The Right! Carolyn made the plaque in Relief Society a year ago and presented it to the family during home evening. Now and then she would remind one of the children of it when asking them to clean their room or mow the lawn. The phone rang. She pulled herself from the chair.

"Hello?"

"Hello, Carolyn? This is Marge. Listen, I'm sorry to be calling at this hour, but we're kind of in a bind."

"That's all right, Marge. What do you need?" Marge was Relief Society president. She had five children. Each month after the spiritual living lesson, she bore her testimony of the gospel and the joy of being a mother in Zion. Motherhood, she told the sisters, was the noblest and most joyous calling a woman could have.

"This is the situation, Carolyn. Trudy Hesser's been in the hospital for three weeks with her gall bladder. She was released today and is back home now. She really needs someone to look in on her once in a while just to see how she's doing. It'll only be for a couple of days and I thought I'd call Zina Tate and Florence Anderson, too."

"I didn't even know that Trudy was in the hospital, Marge. I'll be glad to help out if I can. I've got to take Kevin to the orthodontist tomorrow but that won't be until the afternoon sometime."

"Oh, Carolyn, you're a dear. It would really help us out if you could stop by early tomorrow morning. I'll try to get Zina to take care of it for the afternoon. After you get the kids off to school would be fine."

"Okay, Marge. Tomorrow morning is fine."

"We really do appreciate it, Carolyn. I've called three sisters in the ward already, but you know how it is trying to find someone with the time. I knew we could count on you."

"It won't be any trouble, Marge."

"Just check in to see how she's doing. See if she needs anything. Let her know we're thinking about her."

"Okay, that sounds fine, Marge."

"Thanks again, Carolyn, and I really do apologize for not calling sooner."

"Don't worry about it."

"Well, if you're sure. Thanks. Goodnight, Carolyn."

"Night." She placed the receiver back in the cradle. She knew she would be sick in the morning. She'd been nauseated off and on all day and thrown up three mornings last week. Sometimes when she was pregnant, she got so sick she could hardly move. When Paul or the children came into the bedroom to ask her how she was feeling or if they could get her anything, she had to restrain herself from crying out, "Don't touch me. Go out. Go away." It came in wave upon wave of violent nausea and filled her with festering hostility and sometimes she yelled at the children.

Emma Riggs McKay, in *The Art of Raising Children Peacefully*, had admonished good mothers to refrain from raising their voices. She exhorted mothers to patience and tenderness toward their offspring. Once, when Carolyn had been pregnant with Jennie, she slapped Jeff hard in the face for walking across the freshly mopped kitchen floor

31

with muddy tennis shoes on. Afterwards, nausea churning her insides, she'd gone into the bathroom and thrown up, then come out and apologized to her son. The next day she made his favorite peanut butter brownies for dessert.

She arched her back then gathered up the neat stacks of clothing, being careful not to mix them. Last Sunday in sacrament meeting Bob and Louise Chapman had given talks on parenthood. Louise, who was in her early thirties and had four small sons, reminded the ward members that mothers were co-partners with God in creating new life. In Relief Society during the mother education lesson, she once told the sisters that Bob gave her a special priesthood blessing at the onset of each of her pregnancies and again when she went into labor. The last blessing Paul had given Carolyn was over three years ago when she'd been hospitalized with pneumonia. Carolyn still remembered the sudden, surging comfort that had flowed through her as he had anointed her head with consecrated oil. The next morning her fever was down, the congestion in her lungs cleared. She put the folded clothes away quietly when she entered the sleeping children's bedrooms. She wanted to ask Paul for a special blessing now.

"Hush, David. Quiet, baby." The shrieking started a dull throbbing in her head. "Quiet, Son." Fumbling, she unsnapped the crotch of his sleeper and felt inside his plastic pants. His diaper was dry. Maybe he was hungry. She carried him out to the kitchen. He sucked noisily for a few seconds on a bottle of orange juice, then pushed it away and continued crying. She held him, rocking him for five minutes. Her back ached. Her arms were cramped. The noise pounded against her head and made it throb. "I'm tired, David. Please, please stop crying."

"Mommy, is David mad?"

"What are you doing out of bed, Jennie?"

"I want a glass of water. Will you get me a glass of water?"

"Jennie, you know you can't have water before bed. Remember when you wet the bed last week? Do you want to wet the bed again?"

"But David woke me up and I'm thirsty."

"Go back to bed Jennie." David still cried.

"I'm thirsty."

"No, Jennie. I'm not going to tell you again. Go back to bed."

"I want some water." And she began to whine and rub at her eyes.

Carolyn grabbed her hand and pulled her toward the hall. "I told you to get in bed."

"I want some water." Jennie was crying now. Carolyn stopped. David still screamed. Maybe he was sick.

"All right, Jennie." She heaved a sigh. "All right. Stop crying. You can have a glass of water."

She walked back to the kitchen and filled a plastic cup from the faucet. "Here. Now back to bed."

The little girl drank the water. "I won't wet the bed, Mommy. I promise."

"Good, Jennie. Goodnight."

"Is David thirsty, Mommy? Is that why he's crying?"

"No, Jennie. I don't know why David is crying. It's late. Now go get back in bed."

"Okay, Mommy. Night, night."

"Goodnight, Jennie." Then, sorry for her abruptness, she kissed her free hand and pressed it to the child's forehead. "Mommy loves you. Night, night."

She sank into one of the kitchen chairs, her shoulders and arms and lower back in painful rebellion against the weight of the crying baby. Carolyn remembered the horror stories she had heard about the pioneer women; how they had pulled hand carts when pregnant and delivered babies within the freezing shelter of wagons and tents. The women had large families. Brigham Young said it was the duty of all good Latter-day Saint couples to have as many children as they could. The Lord wanted to send babies to Mormon homes where they could be taught the gospel. Carolyn and Paul had never used birth control except for the year after Susan was born when Carolyn had had some kidney problems. She knew that children didn't come to LDS homes by accident; the Lord sent them. She whispered, "Stop crying, David. Stop crying." Blood pulsed throbbingly through her temples.

She'd been surprised when seventeen months ago Dr. Neilson, smiling, had said, "Carolyn, you're going to have another baby." She was thirty-eight years old and it had been over four years since Jennie was born. She didn't tell Paul for three days. When she'd been pregnant with Jeff, she'd taken a girlish pride and excitement in her condition.

With the others it was more and more a routine discomfort, oftentimes brutal. But with David she was different, obsessed, almost heady with the sense of her womanhood. At night in the dark cool of the bedroom, she would touch her abdomen and trace the curves of her breasts with her fingers and sometimes she thought about God. She was filled with infinite affection for the embryo-child swelling her body and for Paul and the children. During the day she felt an excitement and energy unfamiliar to her. She watched her children with tender awe. Sometimes she wanted to reach out to them, to Jeff and Susan her eldest, and kiss their faces and stroke their hair and press their bodies to her. The backaches had started in the fifth month and then the overwhelming fatigue. She still remembered the strange joy that had slipped suddenly from her.

"Good, baby." David was beginning to quiet, just whimper. She held him for several more minutes until his eyelids began to droop and he drowsed. She filled a glass with water from the sink and took two aspirins from the medicine cupboard and swallowed them. Her head still throbbed though the baby had stopped crying. She switched out the kitchen light and walked back to the nursery to lay David carefully in his crib. Then she continued down the hall, stopping to turn out the bathroom light. The smell of a dirty diaper filled her nostrils. She'd left the diaper earlier to soak in the toilet and then forgotten to rinse it out. David had had diarrhea for two days. He had a sensitive stomach. For five months after he was born, he'd had severe colic. All the children except Kevin and Jennie had had colic. A baby with colic sometimes screamed for hours and nothing could be done to make it stop screaming. David had sometimes lain awake all night crying.

She bent to pick the diaper from the toilet. Suddenly she was sick, nausea flooding through her. Gasping, she rushed to the basin and vomited. She retched into the basin for a long time and afterwards sweat poured from her face and her body was weak and trembling, her hands pale.

David would still be in diapers when this next baby was born.

She rinsed the basin, then turned and rinsed the diaper and dropped it into the plastic diaper pail. She stood for a moment arching her back, waiting for the trembling in her body to stop, then turned off the bathroom light. The phone rang. She walked down the hall to the bedroom.

"Hello?"

"Hi, Honey."

"Hi, Paul."

"Hey, we're kind of tied up here, Carolyn. I just thought I'd call to let you know so you wouldn't worry. I should be home in half an hour. Forty-five minutes at the most."

"That's fine, Paul. Thanks for calling."

"If you're tired, Honey, don't wait up."

"Okay, see you in a little while."

"See you. Bye."

"Bye."

Paul was a thoughtful husband. He always called to let her know when he would be late. Shirley Crandell had married her husband, Ray, in the Logan temple. He was inactive now and Shirley came to church every Sunday with her three sons alone. Carolyn had heard that Ray drank beer and in the winter sometimes took his sons skiing up at Park City on Sundays. Paul was a good father. He would ordain Kevin a deacon next month, and he took the boys and sometimes one of the girls fishing almost every Saturday during the summer. He would be happy to have another baby. When she told him, he would be surprised and glad and would hold her, kissing the top of her head and saying, "That's wonderful, Carolyn. I love you." For several weeks he would be especially considerate, embracing her often and helping with the dinner dishes. He'd always wanted a large family. His mother had ten children and two miscarriages. He would be horrified and hurt if she said to him, "I love you, Paul. I love the children. I don't want another baby." Then screaming, "I can't stand it! Oh God, Paul, please understand! I can't stand it!" In her prayers every night she thanked the Lord that Paul honored his priesthood and then asked the Lord to help her be a more perfect wife.

She sat down on the edge of the kingsize bed and arched her back, then unbuttoned her blouse. Her abdomen was fleshy, her breasts shapeless, sagging. She'd put on ten pounds during her last pregnancy that she hadn't been able to lose. Before they were married, Paul told her that he found overweight women unattractive. Her once slender hips now measured thirty-eight inches.

Stiff with fatigue, she slowly took off her clothes and dressed for bed. Friday she would see Dr. Neilson. He could prescribe a pill for nausea. The digital clock on the nightstand clicked 11:03. David woke up every morning at 5:30 crying to be changed and fed. She rose and folded back the bedcovers and laid Paul's folded pajamas on the dresser top. A framed photo of her and Paul on their wedding day, his arm around her, their smiles radiant, was on the dresser. They stood in white on the Salt Lake temple stair. Dr. Neilson would smile when he told her she was pregnant again. She would ask Paul for a blessing after sacrament meeting this Sunday. And the nurse with the pleasant voice would smile, too, and schedule her for another appointment in one month. A quiver passed through her arms and thighs as she knelt beside the bed to say her prayers. She arched her back.

Bread and Milk

Eileen Gibbons Kump

AMY LOOKED AT HERSELF IN the glass over the washbowl and saw Eve. She couldn't help it. Caught up in her miracle, she would have been offended to remember that her own mother was a bride who had once kept the same astonishing secret.

Amy took the mirror from the wall, stood it against a jar of souring cream, and sat and looked at herself the whole time it takes mutton stew to simmer done. She touched her cheek, her throat, her sleeve. She reached for the sunlight by the window but it was out of reach, warmth on the wood floor. She pretended she dare not go get it. After all, she said to her image, we are going to be a mother.

She said it with her eyes because she could not yet say it with her voice, except to Israel in the darkest, quietest part of night, in a whisper. Even then her voice had been hesitant, and shy. And later, when she thought him asleep, Israel had said, "I saw it, Amy. I knew!"

She had stared toward him through the dark.

"I knew yesterday, by the way you talked. As if—as if you were afraid to breathe. It was like—"

Amy did not hear him finish. Her body numb, she could only lie there betrayed and relive one incredible, enchanted moment. No more than an hour before, uncertain how to tell a thing so fragile, so private, she had considered for one instant never sharing her secret with anyone. Her secret! With morning, intuition could be everywhere!

After Israel was asleep, Amy crept out of bed, tiptoed into the cool room, and shut the door behind her. While she dug a wooden spoon full of firm honey, then let it melt on her tongue, she talked. She told herself that baby having was everyday, like bread and milk. She listened to Papa again: It is the pattern of all life in a world made out of joy and pains.

But could such a thing really be discerned in a voice? And if so, what was a bride to do? Her duty to a husband Amy had understood and accomplished. But to make it known without even meaning to do so, or worse, to acknowledge it by announcing her condition! It seemed as impossible as talking about an unanswered prayer.

The cool room began to chill her. A decision had to be made. Well, if folks knew already, she would try to forgive them. If they didn't, they would not learn it from her. She would tell nobody, and she would remember to breathe when she talked.

Israel said he understood. "But we ought at least to tell your ma," he said more than once in the weeks that followed. They did not. Amy had forgiven him his presumptive eye in exchange for a promise.

And she was happy. To be alive was to be content. Every morning before breakfast, she went with her sweetheart along the trapline to look for red foxes, coyotes, and skunks. She got to weeping over the dead animals, but the strange weeping only increased her happiness.

"Your condition has made you foolish," Israel whispered one morning as they knelt over the trap and its victim. "I ought to leave you home."

But he never did. They drank from the bubbling springs fringed with watercress, they watched the sunrise as they climbed over the hills and through the brush. Evenings they trapped quail, dressed it, and hung it on a string before the hot coals of the fireplace to roast. Over parched corn, roasted apples, and potatoes, they feasted and read and sang and told love stories. And all the time a secret thrived, twice protected; in Israel's heart it was a squirming captive, in Amy's, a friend, cushioned in light.

Lamps burn low, and go out. One Sunday morning Amy could not button her best bodice without a tug. Rushing to the mirror, she saw herself at last. She was not Eve. She was simply pregnant, and it would take a drunk Navee not to see it. Quickly she finished dressing, wrapped a shawl about her, and in her mind resolved to spend the rest of her life in the wood closet. Instead, she sat down and waited for Israel to finish hitching up the wagon. During Sunday school she would think what to do. She would keep her shawl around her and she would think and by evening services, when she stood to lead the singing, she would have an answer.

"Go without me, Israel," she said as he came into the house. But she still wore her shawl and her plea sounded empty even to herself. "Please." Israel took her hands and led her through the door. "This afternoon I'll take you to see your ma."

As they walked into the chapel, he took her hand. "Keep your shawl on, now."

Harriet Taylor put her arms around her daughter and held her. "Bless you," she said. "God bless you both, and now I have a surprise too." She disappeared up the stairs and was back with full arms.

"I will hold it up so you can see."

The mother hubbard was pale yellow, with an endless pattern of tiny black flowers. And it had full sleeves, the fullest Amy had ever seen.

"I was extravagant, Amy, but I couldn't help the sleeves."

Amy looked at it and away. "But Mama—"

"Amy. My dear Amy. Do I need to be told my daughter is going to have a baby? Forgive us. We tried to wait."

"Papa too?"

"Before I could tell Papa, he told me."

"Mama?"

"I think it was the way you walked, as if you were on fall leaves you didn't want to crush. Papa said you kept touching your cheek."

Amy sighed then, sank into a chair to cry, and would not let anyone touch her. Brand new in the world, like a newborn infant herself. That was what she was. And useless. How could she have forgotten that her own mother had had babies, maybe would again? And how could she keep up in a world where people did not need to be told the most secret of all secrets? Worse—oh, far worse—how could she await this baby, then bear it, with everyone watching, and later, helping? She stood up, dried her eyes, and walked to where the mother hubbard lay, a mound of sunlight. She wanted to understand.

"Everybody knows then, don't they. The Roskelleys and the Smiths and the—"

"They don't know, Amy, but they think they do because they expect it. Folks have been waiting."

"Waiting!"

"You have been married five months, you know."

Could it have been that long? Or had it been forever? Well, it did not matter.

"Mama, look at me. How can I stand up tonight in meeting and lead the singing before people who are waiting? How can I stand up there with my arms raised, my middle big, and—"

"Amy!"

"I will look like a washboard!"

"Don't be vain, Amy. Remember—*all women have babies.*"

Amy could not explain nor discard her foolishness, how the thing she could not do was to help.

"I will have to stand up there and be weighed like a sack of grist."

"Yes, child, you will."

Amy stood clutching her shawl about her shoulders with one hand, the baton with the other. All eyes held her. How she had pleaded and coaxed on other Sundays: "Sit up straight, look high, keep up with the baton! Look at *me*." Tonight not one face was toward the songbook in the lap. And everywhere she saw not friends and neighbors but only sinister curiosity. Israel was watching her too, but he was not singing. His favorite hymn and he was forgetting to sing. She clutched her shawl less tightly.

Amy made herself look into the faces, the intent, interested faces, and as she did she smiled. She could not help herself. In fact, if she did not do something right now, she would laugh.

She breathed deep as she tapped the podium with her baton. The music stopped. The voices faded. "Brothers and sisters." The shawl fell to the floor. So they would watch her, would they! So these blessed souls would wait for her to be with child, would they! "Brothers and sisters, you are forgetting that a song is a prayer."

She turned sideways, walked over to the window, and pointed into the black square of outside. "Do you hear the quail? Do you hear its cry? It is lonely. Now for goodness sake, sing as if you are lonely, lonely for the Father."

She walked slowly back to where she had stood, raised both arms high, and began to sing. Her father's face was a flush, her mother's a glow. All she could see of Israel was the top of his head.

40

Pregnant Again

Marni Asplund-Campbell

AN ASTRONOMER SAID SHE could make a map of the universe,
or the nearest part of it, by measuring the light of stars, one by one, re-
cording the flash that reaches earth in a fragment of time. Dividing the
spectrum of the emanation, there is a sudden flash of red, the burst of
hydrogen, that comes when a light source is at a certain distance. She
drew whole systems, galaxies, relative to her fixed lens, perched on a
mountain top, free from the interference of manufactured light. When
she showed her slides, I laughed! Trembling in light, on the pale screen,
the universe was dancing. A million tiny stars, clustered around vast
dark spaces, looked like arms and legs, connecting at the fine tips, bal-
lerinas on point, holding hands, or paper dolls in a bright chain.

> Now I am expecting. I expect many things,
> the fixed points in my life, to move quietly aside.
> First, the wall of an egg compromised
> then my sleep, interrupted
> with bright dreams and heavy breathing.
> My lungs, kidneys, bladder,
> compressed at the edges of my frame,
> our family will shift to receive
> another voice, eyes, expectations.
> I measure this all so carefully
> with small signs, red shifts,
> one day, two days lapsed in a predictable pattern,
> subtle, enormous deviation.
> The days become monumental as I wait
> for a sign,
> the shape and weight of my breasts,

a change no one would know, but me.
From a thought, a smile,
comes first this uncentered weakness,
then stern kicks against my inner skin, a
destructive shaping of hand and forehead,
eyes the color of ice, or chestnuts,
the silent revolution of days,
reminding me of my forgetfulness
in the nearly empty universe,
that I have not felt your hand for centuries.

Delivery

Young Mother

Ila Asplund

In the hospital for over a month,
you've learned a lot about Eating Disorders,
Depression, Dysfunction,
watching talk-shows every day.

The doctor says you must lie down, you
mustn't move. It's silly, you say, and you're
bored. So your mother will kidnap you
from the room full of flowers and gifts
and take you shopping.
In this place you are Queen.
You might have left the veil and ivy
pinned to your coif: it hasn't been long,
and you're still the girl in white.

You are eating a pound of pistachios.
It seems that the salt would absorb
what little fluid is left
around the two boys inside,
the shrinking one's forehead resting
in the growing one's neck—

It's good they will section you early:
no stretching this way, you'll be
back in no time.

Giving Birth: Women's Voices

Lynn Clark Callister[1]

IN A REMOTE MOUNTAIN HIGHLAND, Luz, a tiny Mayan woman, dressed in the colorful woven native dress of her Guatemalan village, speaks of giving birth in her humble home attended by a traditional midwife, shares her perspective that

> I felt that God had given me a gift. It's true that I had to suffer to obtain it, but it is something that God gives.

In a medical center in Turku, Finland, sitting in a comfortable day room filled with light, Maija shares the birth of her son after eight years of infertility:

> It is an experience without words. There are no words to describe this experience. Perhaps only a mother's heart can feel it.

Speaking from her modest student apartment in a college town in the western United States, Christine, a first-time mother, says with deep emotion,

> I couldn't believe what I felt when I saw my daughter born. I have been a Rhodes scholar, but nothing I have ever experienced in my life comes close to what I felt when I gave birth.

In a large frame house where four generations of her husband's family live, Rebecca cradles her newborn son in her arms and says,

> It's a natural phenomenon. If God wanted women to have babies, he gave them the strength to give birth.

Sitting on the floor in her modest home in a Palestinian refugee camp, Amal said the best part of giving birth was to

> see my child. I saw the result of nine months of pregnancy. Seeing my
> son for the first time was an unforgettable experience.

Giving birth is both a process and an event. Because childbirth is a multi-dimensional experience, many variables contribute to the perceptions of a woman about her childbirth experience and the meaning of this event in her life. Among the most significant variables is the societal-cultural context within which the mother gives birth. Because childbirth is an emotional, physical, cognitive, cultural, and potentially spiritual experience, these dimensions cannot be adequately described by quantitative means alone.

In order to tap from the perspective of women the socio-cultural meanings of birth, over the past nine years interviews have been conducted with American Latter-day Saint women, Canadian Orthodox Jewish women, Finnish Lutheran women, Jordanian Muslim women, and Guatemalan Catholic women.[2] These socio-cultural groups represent the three most prominent worldwide belief systems: Christian, Judaic, and Islamic. This essay focuses on those women: the daughters of Eve, the daughters of Sarah, and the daughters of Hagar. In such societies, to varying degrees, a woman's social status is linked to her reproductive role, particularly for the traditional Jewish and Muslim woman.

Asking women to share their birth stories and articulate the meaning of this event engendered rich, descriptive, qualitative data. As women were given the opportunity to share their understanding of the multiple dimensions of giving birth, they constructed their own realities. This was expressed by one Muslim woman: "Each woman speaks from her own experience." There are shared cultural meanings of childbirth as a universal experience for women, but also unique and intensely personal meanings for each woman.[3] Content analysis revealed related patterns of descriptive data bits, called "thematic moments,"[4] which arose from the women's stories. Giving birth represents:

1. **An incredibly significant life event**. For these women birth could either represent a peak experience or simply a means to an end: a difficult passage to motherhood. The Hebrew word for sorrow is *as-*

tav, meaning "to labor," "to sweat," or "to do something very hard." An Orthodox Jewish woman explained the essential connection for her between the bittersweet paradox of sorrow and the joy in giving birth:

> Childbirth is a very painful experience, but what do you get for it? You get something you can't get anywhere else in the world. You get a human being, you give life. It's the most incredible experience in the world.

Some women considered giving birth as a test of personal competence, a coming of age, a sense of power and achievement. A woman experiencing an unmedicated birth shared these thoughts about her experience:

> I was tired but I guess I found my forces each time a contraction came again and again ... If you're strong in your [mind] then that will give you strength to your body.

Mastery was beautifully articulated in this way:

> The experience of childbirth made me grow up a lot. It really did. I've learned a lot about my capacity ... When I thought I was just too tired to push anymore, I found another fifteen minutes worth of it. I just learned I have a lot more strength than I thought I did. Childbirth brought me more in tune with my body because I know what my capacities are: my mental capacity, my strength. I just know I could do a lot more than I thought I could.

2. **A reflection of a woman's personal values about childbearing and childrearing.** The creation of a new family is the hallmark of maturity and self-fulfillment in all cultures, particularly those having codified belief systems related to childbearing. According to one Orthodox Jewish mother, "Life would be nothing without children." A Muslim woman said it this way: "Children are the purpose of life and the happiness of the woman." A Mormon woman described her experience,

> I think it's the greatest paradox of an experience that you can have ... I never experienced that kind of pain in a twenty-four hour period in my whole life, but I never experienced that kind of joy either, so it's definitely pain and joy together in the same circle.

48

This thought is scripturally expressed, "For I have heard a voice as of woman in travail, and the anguish as of her that bringeth forth her first child" (Jer. 4:31). Jesus used the metaphor of the bittersweet mixture of challenge and joy that the childbirth experience reflects: "A woman when she is in travail hath sorrow, because her hour is come; but as soon as she is delivered of the child, she remembers no more the anguish, for joy that a man is born into the world" (John 16:21).

3. **The expression and symbolic actualization of the union of the parents.** For example, the Orthodox Jewish husband, prohibited from observing or touching his wife during labor and birth (*niddah* or law of family purity), if present during birth stood at the head of the birthing bed or stood behind a curtain in the room. Other more conservative husbands did not attend the births, but spoke continual prayers, read passages from the Psalms, or consulted the rabbi. This represented significant and active support for the Orthodox Jewish woman:

> I give birth and my husband helps me spiritually. He can pray for me and that is my biggest support.

The sense of a transformation to a family unit was expressed by a Mormon first-time mother:

> I felt a very strong closeness to my husband because I feel the baby is a part of him and a part of me. Especially that he looks so much like [his father]. I can't even explain it. It's like someone took a string and tied both of us together ... I felt like a unit, a little family.

4. **Obedience to religious law.** For Orthodox Jewish women, giving birth indicates obedience to ancient rabbinical law as recorded in the Torah. According to Jewish literature, "Nothing in life is more wondrous than the process of birth."[5] An Orthodox Jewish woman expressed her perspective that "life would be worth nothing without children."

For Muslim women, giving birth fulfills the scriptural injunctions recorded in the Quran. One Muslim woman said, "People usually start asking you after the first month of marriage whether you 'save anything inside your abdomen' yet, meaning, 'are you pregnant?'"

For Christian women, giving birth fulfills the ancient scriptural texts found in the Old Testament and explicated further, for Mormons, in the Pearl of Great Price, to multiply and replenish the earth (Gen. 1:28; Moses 2:28), spoken of as achieving joy and rejoicing because of the blessing of posterity (Moses 5:11).

Perhaps the linkage with obedience to law is best expressed by this Orthodox Jewish woman:

> This is our life. This is the first commandment in the Torah that we should follow, that you should have children, that you should multiply. First in my life is my family, my way of life, my fulfillment.

One Muslim woman said,

> Our religion encourages us to have children, so I felt I was doing what God was asking me to do.

5. **The creation of life.** Giving birth focuses on the intensity of an incredible experience of co-creating life. The first woman, Eve, was endowed with the title "the mother of all living," which designation preceded her mortal maternity (Moses 4:26). Mothers giving birth love their children as something originating from them and through them. One Finnish mother, speaking of what was the best part of being pregnant for her, said it was

> To know that I was going to have a baby, to feel her kicking inside of me. I couldn't believe that two people could come together and create something like this. It seemed impossible. It was just a miracle.

A Mormon woman expressed a feeling of reverence about participation in the creation of a new life:

> [The best thing about my pregnancy was] knowing that I was going to be trusted with this little person, that Heavenly Father trusted me enough to have her. [It was a] wonderful thing feeling her grow inside of me, [feeling] those feet poke me before she was born.

A Guatemalan mother said,

> [Giving birth] I felt closer to God. I thanked God for allowing me to

have a baby. Well, I don't say she is mine but that he let me borrow her. While the baby was in my womb I realized how great God is. Only God watches over the children that are yet in the womb because only he could do that.

In the interviews, mothers were asked, "What were your feelings when you first saw your baby?" At the time of giving birth, women spoke with tearful emotion of having the sense of the reverence for life itself:

When they laid her in my arms, it was overwhelming ... Suddenly this new child is yours, and you love it so much. [Being a mother means] sacrifice, dedication, and devotion ... but mostly a sense of overwhelming love for your child.

A Finnish woman shared her perspectives of the birth of her first child, a son:

Once he came out, I felt exhilarated. I couldn't believe that the baby came, that the pain would be over. I was crying and laughing at the same time from happiness. I had this flood of emotion. I didn't believe that it was my son.

Muslim women specifically described "the motherhood feeling," a sensation which comes when a woman gives birth. Articulating a beautiful description of her experience during pregnancy, a Muslim woman said,

I felt that the baby and I were joined together, and we were sharing the same dimensions, the same space. So as I was taking care of myself, I was caring for my baby.

Another Muslim woman said,

I marveled about how this miracle could happen. The whole process of creation: How I got pregnant, how I carried my son for nine months, how I became so tired and yet had the strength to finally give birth.

6. **The spirituality of the human experience.** Spirituality is a broad term associated with finding meaning and purpose in life events, which

nurtures wholeness in the individual. It has been suggested that spirituality may be experienced and expressed differently by women than by men.[6] Religious faith or spiritual belief lends perspective to the meaning of life experiences, particularly pivotal events such as childbirth. The meaning of life is connected to the symbolic traditions expressed with cultural/religious heritage.

Giving birth means participation in the processes of life and human existence, knowing that the words health, wholeness, and holiness have the same linguistic roots.[7] Giving birth is one way in which women seek to transcend themselves.

> I finally did something worthwhile in this world. I, everyone, comes here for a purpose, especially the woman. If a woman is going to come to this world and not have children, what was she here for then? She comes here to continue the generations.

A Muslim woman eloquently expressed the spiritual quality of giving birth:

> During childbirth the woman is in the hands of God. Every night during my pregnancy I read from the Holy Quran to the child. When I was in labor I was reading a special paragraph from the Holy Quran about protection. The nurses were crying when they heard what I was reading. I felt like a miracle might happen, that there was something holy around me, protecting me, something beyond the ordinary, a feeling, a spirit about being part of God's creation of a child.

Data reflect the honesty of shared feelings as women spoke in their own voices. There was no reluctance on the part of the participants; they needed little encouragement to talk. There is a yearning in women to experience connectedness with other women through the sharing of significant life events such as giving birth as expressed by one of the women in the study: "I am feeling a real need in my life to learn about women's experiences from other women." As we consider women's ways of knowing,[8] listening to the inner voice and constructed knowledge characterize the articulation of the lived experience of childbirth in the words of these women themselves. One cannot separate knowledge of a life experience such as childbirth from the meaning of the experience itself.

It has been suggested, in woman-centered research, that "women are acknowledged as active, conscious, intentional authors of their own lives."[9] Listening is an essential human skill. The Chinese ideogram for "listening" is composed of the four signs for ears, eyes, heart, and undivided attention. We are invited to listen to the voices of women, to view with respect the sociocultural/spiritual context of women's lives, and to move beyond the superficial to the deeper meanings, sufferings, and joys of the human condition. One writer has suggested that the researcher and participant should be "partners engaged in the ... act of storytelling."[10]

We express our gratitude for the opportunity these women have given us to join in partnership with them in the marvelous experience of interpreting the beauty and uniqueness of their stories of birth. "The deeper personal meanings of childbirth to the woman and her family within the richly diverse framework of her sociocultural/spiritual background should be respected, appreciated and celebrated."[11]

NOTES

1. I appreciate the following departments at Brigham Young University, Provo, Utah, for helping to fund this study: the College of Nursing, the David M. Kennedy Center for International Studies, and the Womens Research Institute; and especially the women who agreed to participate.

2. L. C. Callister, "The Meaning of Childbirth to Mormon Women," *The Journal of Perinatal Education* 1 (1992), 1:50-57; L. C. Callister, "Cultural Meanings of Childbirth," *Journal of Obstetric, Gynecologic, and Neonatal Nursing* 24 (1995), 4:327-31; L. C. Callister, "Giving Birth: Guatemalan Women's Voices," 1997, privately circulated; L. C. Callister, S. Semenic, and J. C. Foster, "Cultural/Spiritual Meanings of Childbirth: A Comparative Study of Canadian Orthodox Jewish and American Mormon Women," 1997, privately circulated; L. C. Callister, K. Vehvilainen-Julkunen, and S. Lauri, "Cultural Perceptions of Childbirth: A Cross-cultural Comparison of Childbearing Women," *Journal of Holistic Nursing* 14 (1996), 1:66-78; L. C. Callister, S. Lauri, and K. Vehvilainen-Julkunen, "Giving Birth in Finland: A Descriptive Study of Finnish Childbearing Practices and Perspectives," 1997, privately circulated; and I. Khalaf and L. C. Callister, "Cultural Meanings of Childbirth: Jordanian Muslim Women," 1997, privately circulated.

3. F. H. Nichols, "The Meaning of the Childbirth Experience: A Review of the Literature," *The Journal of Perinatal Education* 5 (1996), 4:71-77.

4. V. Bergum, "Being a Phenomenological Researcher," in J. M. Morse, ed., *Qualitative Nursing Research: A Contemporary Dialogue.*

5. S. Matzner-Bekerman, *The Jewish Child: Halakhic Perspectives* (New York: KTAV Publishing, 1984), 35.

6. M. A. Burkhardt, "Becoming and Connecting: Elements of Spirituality for Women," *Holistic Nursing Practice* 8 (1994), 4:12-21.

7. E. S. Sorensen, "Religion and Family Health," *Family Science Review* 2 (1989): 303-16.

8. M. F. Belenky, B. M. Clinchy, N. R. Goldberger, and J. M. Tarule, *Women's Ways of Knowing: The Development of Self, Voice, and Mind* (New York: Harper Collins, 1986).

9. S. Brown, J. Lumley, R. Small, and J. Astbury, *Missing Voices: The Experience of Motherhood* (Oxford, Eng.: Oxford University Press, 1994), 5.

10. M. Sandelowski, "Telling Stories: Narrative Approaches in Qualitative Research," *Image* 23 (1991): 161.

11. Callister, "Cultural Meanings of Childbirth," 330.

It Happens So Often

Heidi Hemming Smith

"WOW, WHERE DO YOU PEOPLE come from? You're the fourth one tonight!" quips the emergency room attendant as I ease out of my car into the waiting wheel chair. I do not laugh at his joke. It has been twenty-four hours since I began to give birth to my first child, and finally my contractions are three minutes apart. My eyes wander vaguely over the smooth checked pattern of the floors as they whiz by, and, counter to all birthing class wisdom, I allow myself to imagine that simply entering the hospital doors will hasten the end of this ordeal.

The nurse-midwife checks me and tells me that I can lie in the bathtub if I'd like. My sister Jill spends forty-five minutes with her finger stuck in the little jacuzzi spout that is aimed at my stomach because I can't bear the sensation. A friend is perched on the counter timing contractions while my husband holds my hand and we moan. I close my eyes against the pain.

I am remembering another day. The African sun is baking the top of my head as I follow a fellow Peace Corps volunteer down the rutted, dusty footpath to her village *maternite*—the small cinder block building where all local women are encouraged to have their babies delivered. Gail has mentioned that she is going to help with a young village woman who is in labor, and, having never witnessed a birth, I tag along as if this were a picnic. The smell of mildew and bat dung brings me up short. Passing the recovery room—two women and their tiny arrivals resting on straw mats on the floor—we next find the laboring woman. There is one table in the room, strewn with old medical wrappers and broken glass, but she is kneeling, naked, on the grimy cement floor. Her eyes are glazed over with pain as she looks up and I suddenly feel awkward, like a voyeur caught in the act. I cast about in my mind for something helpful or comforting to say, but I'm still new enough in the country that I only know the vocabulary of everyday situations ... enough to argue over the price of onions, and to ask my neighbors to kindly remove their goat from my garden. An old woman enters and sits, cradling the young woman's head in her lap.

I've heard the war stories ... how when I was born my mother's uterus stopped dilating and the big nurse was pushing on my mother's stomach while the doctor propped his foot up on the table and pulled on the forceps. My father, the physician, always ends this story, "Had you been born fifty years earlier, both you and your mother would have been dead."

Someone forgot to tell me that there isn't always a rest between contractions. They are relentless, one on top of the other. When the nurse-midwife returns from her nap, she says that nothing has changed since she left three hours ago. I think I am going to die.

Standing in the dank hallway, the midwife says matter-of-factly that this labor isn't so bad. After all, this woman is twenty years old and has already borne her husband a couple of children. We've been hovering uncomfortably on the fringes of this drama for about an hour when it begins to rain. The windows have no glass or screen, only big, metal shutters on hinges which we close to keep the water from pooling on the floor. The roof is also metal and the sound is so deafening as to make conversation impossible. The room is completely dark so that we are only conscious of the laboring woman hunched in a corner. When the storm is past, I look at my watch. It is late afternoon and I am a three-hour motorcycle ride from my village. It will be a while before the child is born. On my way out, I stop to touch the hand of a tiny baby the midwife tells us will probably die.

"Unto the woman," he said, "I will greatly multiply thy sorrow and thy conception; in sorrow thou shalt bring forth children ..." In the second day of my labor, this is something of an understatement. When the urge to push finally comes, I am shocked by its violence. My body is a machine—mine (yes, I still feel everything), but also not mine. My great-grandmother did this seventeen times. Countless generations of women perished trying—but this process is so confounding, so extraordinary that I can hardly imagine that I am not the first woman ever to bear a child. Is it really possible that every living being comes this way?

The light of early dawn is in the window. With a final burning shove, he joins us in the world, a small bluish boy with a head of slick, black hair. We are all crying ... sobbing. My arms are so shaky with fatigue and relief that I am afraid I will drop him.

He is healthy, and in his privileged world the odds are in our favor that this will be a long association—perhaps till he's a balding old man. What about that African baby? I don't need to look up infant mortality rates to be reminded that I hardly knew a woman in Mali who hadn't lost a child.

It's another brittle, hot day when we hear that our friend Koro's little sister has died. "How can that be?" my husband and I wonder. She is twelve years old, with budding breasts, and we saw her only last week when we ate with the family. No one really knows what was wrong with her. She just got sick, and a couple of days later. ... This is the first time we have tried to learn the benedictions for the dead, "God save her soul," and "May her resting place be cool." We are not sure how to express our own grief at the news and eventually stumble into the family compound with a tin can full of flowers from our garden. All composure is lost when tears begin to pool in the eyes of the girl's mother.

I have heard it said that women in developing countries must get used to having children die—after all, it happens so often. When I was younger, this argument seemed to me a kind of guilty justification for having so much in an inequitable world. Now I am a mother. Gazing on this beautiful boy who will bear the name of a dear Malian friend, I think of my son's little African counterpart, a child named for my husband. Could it be that when his mother wrapped his tender eighteen-month-old body for the grave, that she thought, "Oh, well, we can always have another one"?

I doubt it.

Mother's Day

Tessa Meyer Santiago

And I told him
Although I hadn't been a fantastic mother,
I sure enjoyed the trip

And
Especially
The part where children become
Friends and people I like to be with

—MERVYL MEYER, May 1985,
speaking to her husband

HER FLOWERS SIT ON THE television still. A pot of white chrysanthemums. I think they died sometime last week, curling brown around the edges. The label says to cut the flowers off and plant them in the early spring, treating them as a perennial. What's a perennial? And it's already June, albeit a cool June. Still I'm not sure June is early spring. So they're still sitting on the television.

It was my first Mother's Day and I lay under the pile of quilts, shivering with breast fever, unable even to get my first legitimate carnation corsage from the elder's quorum. I could hear her moving around the kitchen holding her grandchild in her arms. I hadn't been able to hold Julia for two days. I was sure she had forgotten me and would suffer dire side effects when she reached adolescence. But then I was also sure that she would freeze in her sleep without those four blankets and the quilt the widows from the 13th Ward made her. After all, it was the wettest spring in memory. Mom had once written to me from South

Africa: "My love to you my dearest daughter. I often long for you and wonder what happened to have me miss out on your growing years. Perhaps better this way. I love you." And now she was here, holding my child in her arms while she made Sunday dinner for our small family.

I ate half a potato that afternoon. "Mom, this is one story you never told me about," I complained as she fetched my plate.

"You would never have had a baby, my darling," she replied quite matter-of-factly.

She should know. She had seven.

Motherhood has given me new ways to define pain: one finger, two fingers; and latching onto a cracked, bleeding, engorged breast. All stories I had never heard before.

Whenever I asked my mother-in-law before the birth what labor was like, she smiled and said, "Oh, it's all worth it once you hold that little thing in your arms." I sensed she wasn't telling me something. Mom was really no better help when she arrived. "Oh, my darling, it's been so long, I really can't remember."

But how come their memories cut sharper than a two-edged sword as soon as Julia arrived? Sitting around the dining room table sipping herbal tea, in what resembled an age-old sitting up with the patient ritual, suddenly they remembered. The stories came thick and fast. Suddenly then Mom could remember back thirty-four years, as if it were yesterday, to that little stone cottage which she brought Margo home to. Suddenly she could remember that the doctors had sewn her episiotomy up too far. Suddenly she remembered waiting as long as she could, sometimes three or four days, until she doubled over with cramps, before emptying her bowels. And then, held in my young father's arms, she screamed as the skin ripped apart to let the movement through. And somehow she couldn't quite remember that until 3:00 in the morning when, held in her young American son-in-law's arms, her grandchild clamped down with newborn gusto on my cracked and bleeding nipple.

Why was Ella suddenly so willing to tell me of the time she nursed Scott all day using a special ointment for her nipples which she didn't know made the baby ill? Almost laughing she said: "The more he would nurse, the more he threw up. The more he threw up, the hungrier he got. The hungrier he got, the more ointment I put on my nipples and the more I nursed him. And so we went all day until Frank got home to a screaming baby and a crying wife with bleeding breasts." Perhaps she was laughing because it all happened twenty-eight years ago.

I never laughed. Not once. As each feeding time drew near, the fear rose inside me, like gangrene through a broken limb. I dreaded hearing her start to wake up. In quiet panic I would decide which breast hurt least and unbutton my blouse. I tried to talk to her, not really to say anything, only to fool my husband into thinking I enjoyed this, and also to calm the fear inside. I wanted to be a good mother. Besides, formula cost $6.98 a can; $8.98 if you ran out and had to buy it at Kents. But no amount of appropriate desire in the world could have prepared me for the pain. I can't even describe it. I had never felt such pain in my life. Well, perhaps once, as my father held me down, and a doctor with a large blade lanced an abscess in my armpit without any painkillers. I don't really remember the pain, but to this day I abhor that man.

There was hardly any ecstasy with the agony that this six-pound fourteen-ounce being brought with her. Only pain and more pain, and muscles in my body in spasms. Even when I wasn't feeding her, my breasts were swollen to a dull brick red, purple under the armpits, shiny with fever and infection. There they sat on my chest, immobile, rock hard, hot. And I was supposed to willingly let somebody suck on them. I might as well have attached a vacuum cleaner to my nipples; Julia's suction was just as powerful.

I don't know whether you're supposed to use Lamaze for breast feeding but I did. As Kevin held Julia and pulled my nipple into her mouth, I sat on my hands to stop me from pulling her away. I started singing church hymns to stop the scream and imagined all the pictures on my family's living room wall. My mom collects art, so I could wander through the gallery for at least the forty-five seconds it took for the pain to subside. When I looked down through my tears, I saw a little head nestled against my breast, a mouth sucking my nipple. I was actually feeding a child, my child. These ornaments on my chest that had served so well for decoration before I was married actually had a practical purpose. (The long talks in the bath tub as they rested on my swollen belly must have motivated them to produce—I wasn't sure they knew what to do once the baby arrived so I would talk to the pair periodically to make sure they knew they were up next in the unfolding saga). So perhaps yes, there was ecstasy: that peaceful image, and when she rolled off at the end of the feeding. But most of all, just pain.

It was a pain nobody, no woman had ever told me about. It was as if I had entered this secret society that really knew the truth, but wouldn't tell until you knew it too.

Like the blood that keeps coming out of you for weeks after the birth. Only one woman told me about that: Suzanne Bradley, the basketball coach's wife. She's not Mormon. Maybe that's why she could speak honestly about birth. She didn't have to look at it as "but a sleep and a forgetting," as some church leaders are so fond of quoting Wordsworth to remind us. I wonder if they ever attended the birth of any of their children. I'm not sure their wives were taking a nap through the whole procedure. But I guess Wordsworth was never at his wife's confinement either. Suzanne told me to save all the Maxipad coupons from the Sunday newspaper because I'd be needing them for the next six weeks after the birth. I'd never really thought about how the rest of the fluid inside would get out of me once Julia was gone. She didn't exactly come "trailing clouds of glory"—more like strands of blood and placenta which dripped. For four weeks they dripped. That was a new mother discovery.

Another one I discovered at 3:00 in the morning after I had delivered. I woke up to a burly nurse making bread with my stomach. Over and over she kneaded the folds, punching down the air inside, forcing the fluids out of me. I felt like Julia's green worm in the bathtub: Squeeze him hard and water squirts out his bum. She helped me to my feet. As I stood upright, both legs turned red as the eighteen-inch industrial strength pad between my legs reached saturation point and gave up. Blood splatterpainted the floor like a cheery kindergarten art project. As I shuffled my way to the bathroom, I felt like those old men I've seen in rest homes who wear bathrobes over their clothes and shuffle up and down the linoleum corridors in their slippered feet. "Let's see you go to the bathroom, now," the nurse encouraged me. I never go to the bathroom at 3:00 in the morning, I thought as I tried valiantly to pass wind. Nothing, not the faintest whoosh.

Little did I know that my diet was connected to my bowels' ability to pass gas. They had been put to sleep by the epidural. I think mine stayed asleep. For four days in hospital, a lone styrofoam cup of warm water and a packet of chicken noodle soup graced my lunch tray. Dinner was Jell-O through a straw and a carton of apple juice. "No solid foods until you toot," one nurse reassured me with a smile and a pat on the arm.

I could feel the air bubble inside me. Sometimes it would reach down to my breastbone. Sometimes it would even go as far as my belly button. But for four days it never went past the incision. Nothing was going past that incision. And when it did, my bisected stomach muscles didn't know how to help it on through me. It took weeks before I could pass a bowel movement without tears in my eyes, fists in my stomach trying to ease the pain. No women told me about that either.

Of course, the men were no help. Kevin had already informed me that no pain I ever felt would match the pain in his back from an old basketball injury. In fact, on certain nights he bids me a loving farewell because "People have died from this before, Tess. If I'm not here in the morning, remember I love you." I remind him that he says that every time his back goes out or his nose starts to run. So I don't trust his definition of pain.

I'll never trust a male doctor's definition either. After all, how does a male obstetrician know "this will only hurt a little." He doesn't even have one of his own to find out with. Male obstetrician—the very term defies an empathetic approach.

During labor Dr. Gamette, all 278 pounds of him, comes to check on me. "You're a medical oxymoron, you know," I tell him as I watch his hand disappear into the rubber glove. Suddenly his fingers look very wide and very stiff. All I want to know is whether it's a two-finger or a one-finger inspection. One I can handle with a little squirming. Two is beyond even the best acting. "It's two, but this will only hurt a little," as he snaps the rubber against his hairy wrist that looks as if it could tackle a buffalo on the run. How come it's always the linebacker and not the piano player who decides to be an obstetrician? But, anyway, the fingers are disappearing below the end of the bed to plunge themselves into the very area you were told to guard with your life if necessary. (Better to come home on the stretcher than deflowered.)

Four times in four hours the hand disappears in its antiseptic sheath to check my cervix's dilation. Nothing. Even the pitocin won't induce this child to head down the birth canal. She's lingered in my womb for three extra weeks. The doctor, after the fifth search, says I have a malformed pelvis. I think he calls it cephalopelvic disproportia. To put it simply, my pelvis is square, her head is round. We don't match up very well. If I had been giving birth one hundred years earlier, the medical books would have had the following advice for Dr. Gamette: comfort the mother until she dies. I have a choice: try induction for another twenty-four hours or have a C-section. Twenty-four hours means at least five more missions into the interior. I opt for the C-section.

Twenty minutes later I'm lying on the operating table in a white room with high ceilings. The intern from the paramedics is watching me in case he ever has to do an emergency C-section in an ambulance. He has a moustache. I wonder if facial hair is unsanitary in an operating room. I had a boyfriend with a moustache once. It used to smell slightly of old food. Germs got lost in there quite easily.

The Indian doctor is fixing the epidural tube in my back. She reminds me of the cafe owner on the corner of Main and River, who used to sell me curried meat pies after school. Her accent is comforting. Something familiar in a strange white world. Even Kevin looks like a green creature on a vegetable can. Dr. Gamette is the bishop in our home ward. I'm not sure it's proper for a bishop to have his hands in my womb. I feel like I'm in a scene from a B-grade horror movie: Bishop masquerades as doctor in sacrificial operation. Everything seems to blur together.

They tie my wrists down at the end of my outstretched arms. I can't see anything but the ceiling because they put a large screen in front of my face and an oxygen mask over my mouth. Later, in a haze, I will see bloody sponges flying over the doctors' shoulders, splashing onto the floor. But now I see nothing but the white ceiling. I am scared. I feel the vomit rising in my throat. I want to run away. I fight the urge to gather my arms to my chest to comfort myself. I have visions of my stomach hanging permanently around my knees because they sewed the muscles together backwards. James Walvin's Victorian women with prolapsed uteruses dance in my head. I can hear the whispers from the doorway behind me. It's three grandparents, also dressed in green. My mother has a large nose. She's wearing a hat which pushes her hair flat against her face.

Kevin strokes my hand. "Tell us when you're ready, Tess," the jolly green bishop booms over the screen, "and we'll start." He's pushing on my stomach. Probably stretching it to find a good place to cut. It can't stretch any further than it has. I'm already splitting my skin in silvery streaks all over my hips.

I can feel my toes. I can feel my toes. The fear rises in me. Oh, no, I can feel my toes. I try to wiggle them without anybody noticing. They wiggle. They move. I thought I was supposed to be asleep from the third vertebra down. I can move my toes. I can feel my toes. And he's going to start cutting me very soon. Should I tell them? What should I do? I know I'm going to feel the knife cut me. Maybe I'll just be brave. No, I'm not brave. I'm starting to hyperventilate. I'm starting to cry. I can feel my toes. I bite my lip to hold back the tears.

My mother is standing in the doorway behind me. She's thinking how calm I look. She's so very, very proud of me. I'm biting my lip harder to hold back the tears of terror, readying myself for the cut of the knife.

Just then I hear somebody say, "We have a hand; we have a shoulder; we have a baby." The cut never came.

I can handle the requisite pain of breastfeeding, the agony of broken bowels, the gush of blood and chicken soup for days on end. That's part of a woman's travail. But fear, unnecessary terror and fear: that's not fair. They were already through seven layers of muscle, fat, and tissue by the time I felt my toes. Kevin thought it was the coolest thing he had ever seen. I wish somebody had told me it's okay to feel your toes.

Birth Narratives

Stephanie Smith-Waterman

A FTER I HAD MY BABY, I SAW around me differently. I had this urge (and have indeed done so a few times) to walk up to women and say, "Now I know!" All the children I see around me, and everyone I see, I think, "Some woman had you." It was thoroughly liberating.

I went to the Certified Nurse Midwives and it was an excellent choice for my interactive personality. I felt as if the women talked *with* me, not *at* me. I felt in control, but at one point I realized that the baby was just going to come, whether I liked it or not, and just about then I felt scared.

During most of my hard labor (I got into serious labor at 11:00 p.m., to the hospital at 3:00 a.m., and delivered at 10:00 a.m. the next morning), I had options to try other than just lying in bed, and I found that sitting in the shower was very soothing. At one point the midwife gave me a piece of candy and, to help me through another stage in pushing, grabbed a towel and asked me to do a tug-of-war with her. Things like this may seem silly now, but at the time they were techniques I needed. Especially since I delivered without medication.

My parents were coming for my due date to help us and I had decided I wanted to have both of them there for the delivery. I wasn't sure how it was going to go, and so we left ourselves open for changes in the plan. At one point my dad was actually consoling my husband, Bryan, in the corner while I was surrounded by women at my legs and near my face. I think it eased tension because my dad is really funny, and when I was taking breaks, he told good jokes. So for me it was a great experience. It brought us four and eventually five, including daughter Anna, closer together. One other funny part has to do with the monitor. Everyone somehow turns all their attention to these damnable machines and I hated it. At one point Bryan was watching the contraction

through the wave of numbers and said, "Oh Steph, this is a *big* one."
Out of sheer frustration and anger at that contraption, I yelled, "NO
DUH, BRY!" Everyone got a good laugh.

Arlene Burraston-White

MY FIRST CHILD, A SON, WAS born when I was seventeen. My
obstetrician was and still is a good friend, but the first time I went to see
him, I went because he was an old friend of my young husband's family.
"The whole *family* sees him."

I would never claim to have been "passive," but as a seventeen-year-
old I was somewhat pliable where my doctor went. As my due date
neared, he talked to me about the delivery in general, mentioning that
it would take place at the Dee Hospital in Ogden, Utah. I hit the roof.
Historically, the Dee Hospital had been a tuberculosis hospital. But after TB was under control, it was converted into a regular hospital. I had
been born at the Dee in 1944. But my ear always to the ground, even
as a kid, I'd caught wind of a serious outbreak of staph infections at the
Dee. Several mothers as well as some newborns had contracted staph
there. I told my doctor, "I'll have my baby in the street before I'll go to
the Dee!"

The other hospital in Ogden was Catholic-owned and -operated St.
Benedict's. I told my doctor that I intended to give birth at St. Ben's.
He smiled and said, "Well, you know, Arlene, I have several patients
due around the same time as you. I have privileges at St. Ben's, of
course, but I prefer to deliver at the Mormon hospital and all my patients go there. If I deliver at St. Ben's, I could miss other deliveries at
the Dee."

I snapped, "I don't care—so long as it's not my delivery that you
miss!"

And so on a late Friday afternoon I went into labor. I remember it
was a Friday because my sixteen-year-old husband was the star of the
high school basketball team and they had a Friday night game. He
yelped at me, "Trust you. You would have a baby on a game night!"

And I didn't. Not that I need have worried: I would not have that
child until twenty-seven hours later, in St. Benedict's, my doctor at my
side almost the entire time. But as my husband careened his little white

MG up the hill towards the hospital after that game, as I stared ahead of me at that foreign, to me, neon cross glowing from the hospital, my husband hissed at me, "If that baby is a girl, you can call your parents to take you back home because I won't have either one of you!"

As I rode up in the elevator, sitting in a wheelchair, a white-habit-wearing nun beside me, I was hit with the most powerful sensation I'd ever had to that stage of my life: this was the first thing that had happened to me that I could not control in some way or another. Panic! I said to the nun, "I've changed my mind. I don't want a baby at all." And I was serious. I wanted to get up from that wheelchair and run back down that hill and away from that hospital, and it felt that if I ran fast enough, I could escape. The sweet-faced, soft-spoken nun, stroking my hair, said, "It's too late to change your mind, dear. But you'll be fine—I promise."

There were screams from women up and down the hallways, wending from other labor rooms into mine. I heard women screaming in pain and in anger. "If you ever lay a hand on me again," I recall a woman shrieking at a husband, "I will kill you!" My doctor talked to me with his mouth right up to my ear, to drown the screams out. "You're doing fine, Arlene. I'll stay right here with you. Don't be afraid and don't hear anything beyond you and your own room. Shhh ..."

And I remember all the meals that were served, meals I didn't get. I was starving and weak and knew a breakfast then a lunch had passed along hospital corridors, avoiding me.

I also remember that I had not cried a tear or called out once through all those hours, until just before my doctor decided to take me into the delivery room. I began to weep quietly: "Maybe there's no baby at all," I sobbed to my physician. "Maybe I'll just be here forever, in pain and for nothing ..."

Two hours in delivery and he said, "You have a son!" I cried almost hysterically, tears more of relief than of joy: a boy. Now I wouldn't have to call my parents to take me and my baby home.

Julie Nichols

JACOB WAS CONCEIVED IN A minivan on a camping trip, three years after Jessie was born. Jessie was a terrible baby. She cried all the time, *all the time*. The only reason I didn't send her right back where she came from was because she was a girl (we already had two boys) and having her at home made her unique. Otherwise I'd have returned her and asked for a refund. So when I knew I was pregnant with Jacob—and I knew, I never took a pregnancy test for this one—right away I started talking to him and to God and saying, "I need this baby to be a good baby. Be peace, baby. Be a peaceful baby." We went for long walks up and down the foothills in northeast Provo and I just talked and talked and talked. He was quiet and peaceful in the womb—so much so that I worried a little. But the midwife—who had delivered Jessie, and who was struggling herself with a late-life pregnancy—assured me he was just quiet, that his muscle tone was good, and that all was well.

I went into labor on late Wednesday night. Thursday I called both Brigham Young University and the Waterford School, where I taught part time, and notified my husband and sat around watching television (which I *never* do) all day long. I can't remember when the midwives first came over. As with my first home birth, there were several lay midwives and their apprentices. When Jessie was born, we had eight assistants bustling about. My husband's main impression of that first home birth was of efficiency—even with all those women in the house, order reigned, and after Jessie was born everything was clean and tidy and the women were gone within an hour. My main impression of that first home birth was that, as labor progressed, Diane (the "mother" midwife) walked and talked with me, and when I had a particularly hard contraction, as I was pacing my bedroom, she held me and whispered in my ear till it was over.

It was Friday late afternoon before the midwives needed to come. I was in labor all that time, but not hard, and Diane kept calling. I think she came over once to check me, but she said Jacob wouldn't be born until Friday evening. Which was exactly what happened. She'd done the same with Jessie—had said, "This baby will be born around 8:00 tonight, and will weigh around seven pounds, and I think it will be a girl," and she was right on all three counts.

So late in the afternoon the midwives started arriving. My friend Alda also showed up to take care of my other three little children. The evening wore on. The midwives prepared herbal teas. They massaged the pressure points on the soles of my feet, as well as my perineum. They talked me through contractions—and for the first time I suddenly knew how to make noise to help contractions. I groaned and groaned, and the midwives and the assistants cried, "Yes, yes, that's it, you sound good, very good." My children were afraid, however, so Alda took them downstairs and entertained them.

We had a tape in the boombox of *Fresh Aire* (Mannheim Steamroller). It played for five hours straight, and I hardly even heard it.

About 8:00 the phone rang. It was Diane's husband: her baby, who had been born with multiple problems and was prone to seizures, was having one. With tears in her eyes, Diane leaned over me and begged forgiveness, but she felt that I was in good hands, and she would call one other midwife to come over and preside in her stead, if I could let her go see to her own child (who died a few months later). Thus it was that a complete stranger assisted at Jacob's birth—someone who had never seen me before in her life.

But the first thing she asked after she came into my bedroom and assessed the situation—full dilation, strong contractions, very close together—was whether I'd had an enema. When I said I'd tried to administer one to myself earlier but it hadn't seemed very successful, she marshalled everyone to help me. I was given the enema, and out came the baby, then and there. My husband and three assistants picked me up to get me back to the bed, they sort of flung me horizontal, and the baby slid out slick as you can imagine, two breaths and there he was. My husband had run downstairs to get the other children so they could see the baby being born, but they were asleep, so it took him and Alda a few minutes to wake them, and by the time they were back upstairs Jacob was resting on the bed between my legs and I'd checked his sex and the length of his fingers and the gray umbilical cord lay there throbbing. My husband got to cut the cord, as he had Jessie's, but he missed the actual birth, which was something we were both a little sad about. The children stood around in awe, and my second boy was too shy to hold his slimy little brother, but the other two couldn't wait—the assistants wrapped him naked in a blanket and they held him reverently. Jacob was a little bit gray—it took him a while to find out he was out of the womb—and I said, "Cry, baby!" till he did. Then we put him to the breast and he lay between us all night long, never making a sound.

He was the quietest child we had. He lay in our arms as if listening to the universe. When I brought him in the shower with me as he grew, he lay quiet along my front—never squirmed or fought. But it wasn't because anything was wrong (he's a great little skier these days, with plenty of eight-year-old energy), it was because he knew I needed a peaceful baby.

What was remarkable was the encouragement and accurate assessment of the midwives; the way I could go with the contractions both in my groanings and in my pushing, as I had never been able to do with my other three births; and the way Jacob responded to my talking to him in the womb.

From <u>Salvador</u>

Margaret Blair Young

LUISA WAS CADAVEROUS. ALL of her life seemed centered in that great fruit. Her eyes were sunken, her face bloodless. I thought she was unconscious when I entered the bedroom.

Johnny had gone for the midwife. Dad was who-knows-where. It was just the women in the room now, and the premature event.

"You're doing fine," Mom whispered to Luisa's inert arms.

Luisa's eyes fluttered open. One side of her mouth turned up as if caught on a fishhook. She made a sound like a hoarse cat—a long, painful sound, as limp as the rest of her.

"Over in a second," Mom said. "I know, Cookie. It hurts. Babies hurt."

Luisa drew out her groan until it was a long, thin mew. She went flaccid. Instinctively I put my hand over her heart. She covered my palm with hers. She said something I couldn't hear, and I put my ear to her mouth. Her hand came around my head, cold and limp as death. "My gardenias," she said.

"They're fine," I whispered. "Guzzling mango juice. Doing great. I fed them today."

She lifted her lip into that lopsided grimace, her eyes still closed.

Mom told me the pains were about fifteen minutes apart. Hard labor was a long way off, she said, but things had started. Luisa's water had broken; there was no going back now.

I could not imagine that this wilted body on the bed could really accomplish delivery. Luisa would die and the baby would be pulled from her like entrails from a chicken. Dead.

I thought an unaimed prayer: "Come on. Come on. Be."

Mom told me to moisten a washrag with cool water and put it across Luisa's forehead. "You've never seen sweat till you've seen a delivery," Mom said. "Five weeks early. That's not so bad. Lots of babies are five weeks early, right?"

Luisa mewed.

"You're tired, aren't you, Cookie," Mom said to her. "Rest. You'll need your strength for pushing. Sleep if you can."

There were tears in the corners of Luisa's eyes, glittering under her lashes. I dabbed them with the washrag, then folded and smoothed it over her forehead. She made a quivery noise, a rattling in her throat, like something from an ancient ritual.

"You're fine, Cookie," Mom repeated. "There is nothing on earth lovelier or harder than labor. Oh I know that. Scares the crap out of you when it's you delivering, but brings you closer to the veil than the grittiest prayer you'll ever make."

Luisa murmured, "Yes."

Mom stroked the washrag over Luisa's brow. She said, "Some people say there's a light in the room when a baby comes, like the angels are doing escort service. I want to see about that. I want the lights out so I can see if there's some trail of glory from Heaven. Doesn't that sound tremendous? A glacier of light for the kid's spirit to slide down. Angels holding his hands. Gotta see it."

Luisa moved her head.

"Oh yeah. It'll be wonderful," said Mom. "Old Boinky here, he's probably saying 'bye bye' to all his friends right now. He's probably watching us this very minute. I imagine he's a little uneasy about getting born too. A little scared of how he's going to get that body of his out." She made her voice childlike. "You nervous, Boinky? A teeny bit frightened? Now don't you worry. Everything's set up just like it should be. Your Aunt Em and cousin Digs are right here to meet you. Things are fine. Just fine." Back to normal: "Now Cookie, do you feel like you can sleep?"

"You might need to stop talking before she'll sleep, Mom," I said. I was the one sweating.

"Am I bothering you, Cookie?"

"No." Almost inaudible.

"I'll shut up and let you sleep," Mom said. "Sleep between the pains if you can. That's it."

Mom seemed half-oblivious to the possibility of tragedy. Not that I would have expected otherwise. But I knew she wasn't an idiot. Somewhere in that orange optimism of hers there had to be fears. She couldn't be blind to Luisa's diminishment.

Luisa tensed and let out an exhausted whine of pain. Her head moved from side to side on her pillow. The washrag slipped off her forehead. I took it and wiped her cheeks and neck. Mom held Luisa's feet, as if that would sturdy her. "Breathe through your nose, Cookie," Mom said. "Like your tummy is a balloon and you're going to blow it up. Come on, now, Cookie, breathe with me." Mom inhaled deep. Her mouth was a pucker, her eyebrows lifted high. "Again. Breath with me, Honey." Luisa opened terrified eyes. She obeyed. Her mouth was shaking as she copied the pucker. It shook through all her breaths. Her knees shook too. Mom pressed harder on her feet. Luisa went limp again, closed her eyes, moaned, "Over."

Mom patted Luisa's ankles. "Good job. Damn, you're good. Oh, what am I saying? There are probably a hundred angels around us here, and off I go using my mouth. God should really strike me mute sometimes. I mean that. He really should. Oh, but you were perfect, Cookie! You see how it works? Just like blowing up a balloon. Oh yeah. You're going to do great." She looked at her watch and glanced at the bedroom door. "How far is that *aldea* where the midwife lives?" she asked. Trying to act casual.

"Not far," Luisa managed.

"Well those rascals," Mom said. "They've probably stopped for a soda pop or a taco. Did they think we were kidding about this labor stuff? Those rapscallions!" She laughed, but shot me a quick, desperate look.

"I'll check if I can see them coming," I said.

The curtains were drawn and the kitchen lights dangled brilliantly. I had no clue to what was waiting outside until I opened the front door. There was a slide of lights out there. I gasped and thought "fire" and then "angels" until I realized what it was: the Zarahemlites and their neighbors were holding a candlelight vigil for Luisa. A group of women—women Mom and I had romped with in the stream as they washed; the processing woman; the egg-sorter woman; anonymous women I had seen at the marketplace—about a dozen of them—were kneeling reverently a little distance from the cabin. Others—hundreds of others—were coming to join the prayers, two by two, holding long, white candles. They were coming in utter silence, though a few of the kneeling ones were counting beads. Their rows of candles shone like an ascending runway. All around them, hardly distinguishable, were fireflies; above them stars. This was a light show.

The nearest ones saw me. A couple of the women I had worked with gave me knowing smiles, though none broke the stillness.

I watched the trail of candles zigzag around trees and chicken coops. Two by two, the faces above the candles appeared. Each light moved slowly downward as its holder knelt. Within five minutes there was a magnificent throng of candles and brown faces. Mostly women, but one or two men.

I held up both my hands in a gesture of thanks. They were watching me expectantly. With my hands up like that, it seemed I was ready to give a message. I did not want to talk, their reverence was so moving, but they were waiting for my news.

I said, "*Nada.*" I meant that nothing had happened yet. It sounded, I know, like a statement of nihilism, full of pessimism. But it was the best I could do with my Spanish. "*Nada. Gracias.*"

Their faces were devoted. I wondered if Johnny had any idea how much they loved their Luisa. I suspected he did.

I repeated "*Gracias*" several times, until the jeep lights appeared at the rim of the hill.

Johnny had to have seen the candles. He flashed his headlights on and off several times, like the Woodward Avenue bus driver had done to tell me hello from his distance.

The crowd turned its collective face to the lights. Johnny revved the engine. The jeep could be loud with some prodding from the gas pedal. It made the kind of VARROOM little kids imitate with toy race cars. A good, long, high-speed noise that seemed to echo off the hills to signal an earthquake or heavenly visitation; a noise like rushing waters or a crackling wind. The people watched the roaring lights come over the hill and through the same zigzag they had just negotiated. Johnny honked, flashed his brights, pulled up next to them. The midwife had arrived.

The candles made her face quite visible as she got out of the jeep. It was the most wrinkled face I had ever seen. More wrinkled, even, than Primitivo's. It was a study in oval: the face shape itself was oval, as were the wrinkles extending from forehead to chin, and those around her baggy eyes and around her flaccid cheeks. She had a set of the most incredible jowls I had ever seen on man, woman, or dog.

She grinned. She had no teeth that I could see. As I had done, she held up both her hands. But where my message had been impotent, hers was full of power: it was herself, her merciful arrival, her ancient, victorious presence. She was wearing several black shawls with long fringes. As she lifted her arms she looked magical and bird-like—something you'd expect on Halloween. She cackled too, like a happy, benevolent witch. Thrilled to be on hand for the Gringos.

The people smiled gratefully, watched as she went inside—limping and hunchbacked but energetic still—with Uncle Johnny. Then they returned to their prayers.

Inside the cabin, Johnny was boiling water and noisily sorting out medical instruments; Mom was going in and out of the bedroom, doing miscellaneous tasks like unfolding blankets and fluffing pillows; the midwife was happily—laughingly at times—barking out instructions in a mix of Spanish and her shrill dialect.

I asked Mom how I could help. She told me to wet the washcloth again. I took it from Luisa's forehead, telling her as I did about the women outside. She gave a vague nod. "Our way," she said.

"So how far apart are the pains?" I asked Mom.

"Ten minutes. She's doing great."

Mom hadn't reapplied her lipstick in hours. It was flaky and creased in her pucker lines. I noticed, too, that she had some silver hairs. I had forgotten she dyed her hair.

The midwife was taking Luisa's clothes off. Luisa was a rag doll, willing but lifeless. When at last she was naked, the disproportion between her thin arms and legs and that full, stretched stomach was grotesque.

The midwife put her ear on Luisa's navel, then cupped her hands around the solid lump of her middle. She seemed to be measuring the child. Luisa groaned. Again the midwife measured and again, as though she were not satisfied. Then she stood and proudly announced, "*Hay dos.*"

"Twins," Mom gasped. "Oh hell." For the first time, her composure was gone. She turned her face so Luisa wouldn't see, and pressed her eyes. Of course, when she turned back a few seconds later, she was beaming like a bride. "Two for the price of one," she gushed.

"Price," moaned Luisa.

"Twins! How about that, Cookie? Hey, did you hear how I understood that Spanish? You're a good teacher. The best."

The midwife was silly with mirth. I could not understand a word she said, but she seemed to be teasing Luisa. She talked incessantly, laughing, gesturing, smiling patronizingly through all her instructions as though she were addressing the babies, not their mother. I would have thought her senile if I hadn't watched her hands working over Luisa's crotch. Those wrinkled hands were expert and agile. They massaged Luisa's thighs and perineal muscles, then made a circle that indicated how big Luisa would have to get before the birth could proceed. Through all of this, she chattered gleefully on and on. Sometimes, between pains, she demanded that Luisa respond to her teasing. She displayed her pink gums and repeated insistently, "Eh? Eh? Eh?" until Luisa gave an answer, however weak. During the pains themselves, Mom breathed with Luisa. The midwife observed this enthusiastically, opening her eyes wide, clapping her hands, exclaiming, *"Buenissimo!"* and *"Que mujer!"*

Johnny came in and laughed right along with the old lady. They were affectionately mocking the delivery, joking about the thinness of the cervix and the veil.

But this birthing didn't stay pleasant. Sometime late into the labor, the midwife measured Luisa's opening and made a futile gesture with her hands. The night was half over, the pains almost continuous, and dilation had stopped. The midwife changed her expression from glee to anger so abruptly it was melodramatic, manic-depressive. She scolded Luisa for her smallness, shook her finger and spoke sharply.

Luisa's eyes rolled back in her head. She said, *"Padre Nuestro que estas en los Cielos, santificado sea tu nombre."*

The Lord's Prayer. She was reciting it like a catechism.

"Hagase tu voluntad como en el cielo asi tambien en la tierra."

Her fingers were moving on her chest, counting invisible rosary beads. She was reverting to a Catholic right there in the childbed. She cried as she recited.

"El pan nuestro de cada dia, da nos lo hoy, y perdonanos nuestras deudas como tambien nosotros perdonamos a nuestros duedores."

Barely audible. A whimper. A plea. Johnny's expression changed too, from amusement to a sublime tenderness only he could manufacture. None of this was bothering him. He could watch her decompose, I thought, and get loving inspiration from her bones. I hated him.

"*Y no nos metes en tentacion, mas libranos del mal, porque tuyo es el reino y el poder y la gloria por todos los siglos, amen.*"

Her eyes shut tighter. Her naked stomach moved, tightened.

"*Ay Dios!*" she said. "*Madre Maria, ayudame.*" She whimpered, gave two little sobs, calling again and again on the Virgin.

The midwife was making vigorous circles where the babies would emerge. Her face was grave. There was no teasing now.

Mom took Luisa's left hand (Johnny was holding her right one) and said, "We're here, Cookie. You've got to get your strength up. Come on, now. You're going to do just fine. We're all with you."

Like the whole lot of us would stand guard. No angel of death would wrap her up with us beside her.

"It'll be over soon," said Mom. "Oh I know this hurts. Cookie, I've been there. I know."

"Luisa," said Johnny, "Luisa, sweetheart, I've loved you—loved you with all my heart. It's been worth it."

Luisa panted, sighed, and let her head fall sideways on the pillow. Her eyes were glazed and half-open.

Mom patted her hand. "Come on," she shouted, trying, as it were, to scream into the next world. "Come on, Cookie! Almost done! Everything's fine!"

Luisa did not respond.

I watched the scene as if from a great distance, as if I were under water. Everyone seemed frozen, bending over the still, pregnant body. All the faces but Luisa's were full of pity and anguish. Luisa's had no expression. I thought, now they'll cut into her and take the babies out. They'll use one of the knives Johnny boiled. Luisa is dead, I thought, and Mom is a compulsive liar.

Unconsciously I was moving toward the bedroom door. I heard the knocking outside like thunder. I went to it numbly, half expecting to find a faceless, black-robed figure pointing his scythe at the bedroom. The invited guest.

It wasn't Death, it was Dad. Beside him were Alberto, Piggott, and a Latin guy with soft, gentle eyes who I somehow knew was Daniel Castillo.

I said, "You're too late."

Piggott moved me out of his way and strode into the bedroom. Daniel Castillo went behind him. I watched from the kitchen as Daniel anointed Luisa's head with oil. Piggott gave a long, inaudible blessing. His hands seemed much larger than Luisa's head. Someone who didn't know the Mormon ways might think he was slowly crushing her skull.

"No good," I said. "Too late."

"Julie," said Alberto. (How long since he had called me that?) "Julie, remember: you must awake your faith."

Luisa's hand moved.

"You see," said Alberto, "the statue comes to life."

"Alive," I murmured.

Dad whispered. "She was just asleep. Women sleep before the last stage."

"I wouldn't be too certain, sir," said Alberto.

"Well, son," whispered Dad, "as you might have heard, uncertainty is one of my pastimes."

We watched Luisa through the bedroom door. Her face went tight. Dad said, "Here it comes."

She cried out *"Jesus!"* pronouncing it "Hey Zeus"—like she was calling to Mount Olympus. Her mouth stretched into a grimace. She growled.

"Hombres afuera," said the midwife, shooing Piggott, Johnny, and Daniel Castillo into the kitchen. Then to Luisa, *"EMPUJA!"*

The bedroom door shut behind them. There were two separate worlds now.

"Do you want to go in?" Dad said to me.

"Pretty gory, isn't it?" I said.

"Go on in," he said. "They might need you."

I did. Luisa was sitting on the bed. Mom was bracing her, hoisting her up from the armpits. Together they were breathing sharply. The midwife grabbed my arm and put me on the side of the bed. It was my job to bring Luisa's knees to her chest when the midwife said, *"Ahora."*

"Ahora!" I pushed the knees into the chest and mom pushed in on the shoulders. Luisa screamed and bore down.

"*No!*" shouted the midwife. Luisa, she said, was making too much noise. The midwife mimicked her. "*No como una cochina,*" she insisted, making pig noises as though she could humiliate Luisa into proper labor. "*Asi. Asi.*" The old lady modelled the way to push a baby out. She clenched her fists and held her breath. Even her incredible wrinkles seemed to tighten. Luisa went purple with her soundless imitation. The midwife nodded, rewarding her with a satisfied smile. Luisa tried to smile back; her teeth were chattering uncontrollably.

"*Ahora!*" said the midwife.

I think I will never hear the word again without hearing earthy, bestial, strangled breaths of a woman in labor.

"*Ahora.*" It went on for nearly an hour, the midwife mimicking, shouting, scolding, mocking, teasing, laughing, shrieking. "*Ahora!*" Then Luisa gave us a look of terror, a wide-mouthed, wide-eyed look like the mask of tragedy. She panted a high-pitched "*Ya, ya, ya.*" The first baby's head, guided by the midwife, was born. It came out bloody and compressed and seemed to blossom in the midwife's hands. Two more pushes, and the rest of the body emerged. A boy—tiny, unnaturally wrinkled and red, but very much alive. He gave a lusty wail and peed onto the midwife's chest.

Luisa fell back into Mom's arms. Mom lowered her to the pillow and let her rest until the next set of pushes began, about fifteen minutes later. The second baby was a boy as well. He peed on his mother as the midwife held him up.

Mom shouted to the closed door, "John, you're the father of twin boys!"

John yelled the news to the crowd outside. We heard him, and his echo: "*Gemelos! Varoncitos!*" We heard the applause of the Zarahemlites too, like a rainstorm.

Luisa lifted her arms. She was still shaking. Mom held one boy and I held the other against her breasts. Luisa sobbed and brushed her finger across her babies' cheeks.

"Oh damn!" Mom said then. "I can't believe what an idiot I am. I left the lights on, can you believe it? Why there could have been angels tap dancing on the bed. There could have been a whole aurora borealis on the ceiling, and I had to go and leave the damn lights on! Can you believe it? I may not see angels again till I die. Damn!"

My Sisters, My Daughters

Martha Sonntag Bradley

I *ALWAYS WANTED A SISTER,* but I got three brothers, one
with blond hair, one with black, and one I liked to pretend was my
twin. So the fact that I gave birth to four daughters and two sons was
a particular joy. I was bitterly disappointed when my grandmother told
me that my third brother was in fact a boy and not a girl. We were
sleeping together in my parents' four-poster bed, snuggled beneath
heavy patchwork quilts, moonlight dancing in through the window
over our shoulders, when the phone rang. I knew it was the hospital.
And I was just as sure that it was news of my sister's coming.

When my grandmother returned to the bed, she turned to me, gathered me into her arms, and said, "You have another baby brother." I
cried noisily and sloppily, breathless, heaving sobs into her shoulder
long into the night. I imagined that I would wander lonely and misun-
derstood my whole life without a sister in whom to confide. My unfor-
tunate beautiful black curly headed brother Peter appeared as often as
not in frilly dresses in photos taken long into his third year. In all his
baby pictures he looks like my baby sister. But his sweaty little boy
smells and scabbed up knees belied my efforts at re-creation.

I have always looked at families of sisters with envy, tracking their
bonding and shared lives as proof of what I've missed. So when I had
daughters, four of them, I knew the value of what I had been given—a
female circle of my own, in my home, that I could watch and experience firsthand as it defined and re-defined itself. The circle I experienced began with my grandmother, wove through my mother to me,
through me to my daughters, a flower wreath woven together with
vines, leaves, petals of different hues and textures.

I have a photograph of my grandmother, my mother, and me that I
keep in my desk. My grandmother was a big woman who stood tall and

true. Her character is painted on her face with the strength of Utah and the hope of the Mormon pioneers. Still, she was a common woman, a woman who worked her entire life. I was crazy about her.

My mother stands in front of her, a far more diminutive figure. She has a tentative, hopeful look on her pretty face, and she is holding her daughter, me, up for all to see. This was her hope for future good. The stubborn, spoiled look on my two-year-old face tells you also where I fit into this threesome. I have searched our faces endlessly for meaning, what bound us together, what threads through us still.

My grandfather was a sheepherder who lived most of the year in southern Utah in the desert. When my grandmother married him, he had three older children. They needed a mother, she was a good woman. It was not a marriage based on love and affection but a practical accommodation to both of their needs. My grandmother had never had her own baby, and when she was forty-five years old she traveled to Salt Lake City, visited an orphanage, and picked out two babies—my uncle Howard and my mother. That night she went to a Hawaiian vaudeville show and took the name of the heroine of the vaudeville show for her daughter—Luonna.

My grandmother was a good mother, kind and broad-hearted, but because they were poor, she was not always able to stay at home with my mother. When my mother was eight years old, she had rheumatic fever and for two years stayed in bed at home alone while my grandmother worked in someone else's home. Mother spent her second and third grade years in a four-poster bed filling a scrapbook with cut-out figures and creating a complicated make-believe world. For a period of time, my grandmother worked as a housekeeper for the home of a prominent senator five days of the week and only came home on weekends. My mother and her brother lived alone in her absence, cooking and cleaning the house themselves.

During that time my uncle and his friends started to abuse my mother, beating her in their mother's absence, mercilessly torturing her, terrorizing her with tales of thieves, robbers, and murder, threats of what they would do if she ever told anyone. Because she was a little girl, mother took this, perhaps believing she deserved it. No one stopped it. No one even knew. Furthermore, whenever my grandfather came into town he would introduce my mother as his bastard daughter, the daughter that wasn't really his, as if she were some toy or animal my grandmother had taken on. I have imagined her crestfallen face at such moments, watching the family from the periphery, wondering where she fit in.

This cycle of abuse filled my mother with demons that she eventually mastered. The fact that my mother broke out of that cycle of abuse, found peace, and became the good kind-hearted woman she is, is a testimony to the strength of the human spirit in the face of adversity. I most admire her for her strength in freeing herself from her past. She is a small woman but heroic in stature in my eyes. My mother's life will be remembered for the good she has done. In fact, I have always thought that my mother's funeral will be something like a circus, stray dogs (which I do not mean in an insulting way), but people she brought into our circle because they had none of their own, whom she gave her clothes to, or her furniture, her money, whatever she had so generously and selflessly to help them feel better about themselves, to get a start, to succeed.

When my mother speaks of my own birth or my childhood, she is somewhat or somehow detached or separated from the events, from the experiencing of me. "We were so rigid then, so bound by Dr. Spock's rules." She says. "I never enjoyed you." So I have a limited sense of connectedness to my mother through my birth.

Nevertheless, I acknowledge what I carry from her. The poet Chungmi Kim wrote a dialogue in which she tells her mother, who lies dying in her bed, of the importance she had played in her life. The Mother says: "I prayed God, I prayed Buddha, to take my life away instead of my children. God and Buddha they left me long ago when the war broke. But nothing matters, nothing." The daughter says: "It matters, Mother. It matters that you are my mother. Through you I had a vision of life different from yours. Through you I learned the wisdom to seek for freedom. You paved the way for my journey into the world unknown. Through you I gained the courage to survive. It matters that I am your daughter. Mirror to mirror through myself I see you. You see me." Like my mother and grandmother, I have not always had a particularly easy life, but from them I inherited strength, intelligence, wit, competence, the ability to stand up again and again after being beaten down. In short, the tools with which to face life with dignity. It matters that my mother was my mother. It matters that my grandmother was her mother. Their journeys are in me, are a part of me.

My grandmother, Vinnie Mae, told me stories, which expressed her philosophy of life, though I often did not recognize them as that. She told me about her relatives, about the skies above southern Utah. Vinnie told me stories about herself, about her mother, about her father, about the midwife twins Martha and Elizabeth from whom I inherited my names. Slipping one day she told me the story of her first husband, the dark and handsome gentile—Berl, the love of her life who had been killed in the youth of their marriage. In this she taught me that life is a circle and everything has a place in it. And that life is what we make of it.

In all of our stories, my daughters, my mother, her mother, and me, we vacillate between being dependent and strong, self-reliant and powerless, strongly motivated and hopelessly insecure. Actors and victims. Paradox runs through our lives like a ribbon. We live with a variety of conflicting feelings and suppressed desires. We resolve this dilemma in various ways, but this paradoxical nature plagues every move we make.

Besides recognizing and acknowledging the significance of each moment in the search for understanding, we must also search for meaning in the connections we have to those who have moved before us and those who follow us, regardless of the shape they take on. Mothering is modeled for us by those who raise us. And much of who we are runs in the blood. I appreciate the connection that runs back through time to my mother and grandmother, and forward to my daughters and their daughters. In Anne Sexton's words:

> I stand in the ring
> in the dead city
> and tie on the red shoes ...
> They are not mine,
> they are my mother's
> her mother's before,
> handed down like an heirloom
> but hidden like shameful letters.

My mother and grandmother were each women who lived marginalized lives yet they triumphed. I remember in Terry Tempest Williams's book, *Refuge*, a letter from Terry's mother to a dying friend where she said, "He [speaking of God] gave me the gifts of faith, hope, strength, love, and a joy and peace I had never felt before. These gifts were my miracle. I know that it is not the trials we are given but how we react to these trials that matters." And so in a very real sense they provided me with a model for confronting life.

There is a scene at the beginning of the play *Angels in America* when Rabbi Usudir Cgenekwutz, of the Bronx Home for Aged Hebrews, pays his respects at the passing of Sarah Ironson, a member of his flock; devoted wife of Benjamin Ironson; loving and caring mother of her sons, Morris, Abraham, and Samuel, and her daughters, Esther and Rachel; beloved grandmother.

As he speaks, he says that although he did not know this specific woman even still he knows her. In some ways she was the metaphor for the American experience. She was all of us. He says: she was

> not a person but a whole kind of person, the ones who crossed the ocean, who brought with us to America the villages of Russia and Lithuania—and how we struggled, and how we fought, for the family, for the Jewish home, so that you would not grow up here, in this strange place, in the melting pot where nothing melted. Descendants of this immigrant woman, you do not grow up in America, you and your children and their children with the goyische names. You do not live in America. No such place exists. Your clay is the clay of some Litvak shetetl, your air the air of the steppes—because she carried the old world on her back across the ocean, in a boat, and she put it down on Grand Concourse Avenue, or in Flatbush, and she worked that earth into your bones, and you pass it to your children, this ancient, ancient culture and home.
>
> You can never make that crossing that she made, for such Great Voyages in this world do not any more exist. But every day of your lives the miles that voyage between that place and this one you cross. Every day. You understand me? In you that journey is.

In the same way my mother's and grandmother's journeys are in me, they form my decisions, my attitude about problems, how to work through them. My delight at the sunrise is in part shaped by their responses to the world.

When I grew up, my sense of self reflected membership in a tribe. Being a Sonntag meant something very specific. We were strong-minded and willful, often funny, always loyal, and fiercely devoted to one another. Because my father had eleven brothers and sisters, there were a lot of us. Everyone I met, it seemed, knew one or another of my Sonntag uncles or aunts or cousins, and that was always a relief because that meant they knew who I was.

My self-identity also reflected my position in my family. The oldest child and only daughter meant I had a privileged position, I was treated differently. Much was expected of me. It was assumed that I would be successful, always try hard, and do my best. And I think I very early on began in perhaps a warped way to think I was the center of the universe. Of my universe that was true. While outwardly I was loud and silly, gregarious and bright, inwardly I was intensely private and melancholy. My interior world became easily the most interesting and comfortable place to reside. The only place I truly felt safe.

I vividly remember the births of my own children. I never felt so connected to my body or as relevant as when I was pregnant, involved in the creation of another. My early attitude toward mothering, when I was twenty years old and preparing for my first son, was identifying a certain body of information, knowledge about what I would do. I had had limited experience babysitting, was unparalleled in my lack of patience with my own brothers, and did not have what I considered the requisite skills at diaper changing, bathing, and so forth. Now I know that adaptability, the ability to bend, and good humor are far more important than technique. Patience is easy with children who so delight and amuse you, inspire you with their bright minds and hearts. I had no sense at twenty of the long haul, that mothering did not have an ending point. These people will always be ours, ours to worry and care about, share our pain and joy with.

I also at twenty had no idea that the rewards were boundless, that the opportunities for service would refine me. That these babies would become my best friends and companions; that quickly they would become smart and funny and that I would crave their company more than anything else.

I didn't know they would be all so different. You sort of assume when you marry and create a combined gene pool that the combinations are limited, that a certain sameness will run through your house. But that is so far from how it plays out. I learned from my children the miracle of variety through the shades of changing moods, hair color and hands, varied gifts and talents, interests and energy.

In some ways the most important memories I have as a mother are of moments so fleeting they are like sunshine moving across the water. There are some moments so potent, so filled with joy, that they sweep you away, bump you off your feet. Some of these things were absolutely ordinary events or patterns repeated daily for a period of days, or weeks, or years. Yet those times are also the reasons mothering is worth all the sacrifice and sorrow it costs.

Each time you birth a child, you set yourself up for incredible loss and perhaps pain. If you're lucky, your experience will be joyful. But it is not a given. Rather, because our children are like us, truly human, we experience with them the complexity of life in all its varieties. With each child it seems we have to learn the rules all over again, to make sense of things. Each time we are faced with different forces and challenges, personalities, strengths, and weaknesses.

It is interesting to me how many of my most acute memories of my children are of them in motion—the way Katelyn looked running across the field after a morning of kindergarten, yellow hair flying around her head like a dandelion crown, filled me with absolute perceptible joy. Emily learning to ride a bike. Surprisingly I remember best watching her ride off, pigtails flopping horizontally from the sides of her head, her little legs pumping vigorously to move her away, around and around the block. Again Emily, at five, stubbornly riding the ski lift all by herself, hugging tightly to the bar but convinced absolutely she could do anything better by herself.

I have learned new things about mothering from my adult children, about how much it defines me. The enormous relief I feel when my daughter Rachael comes home from college in Boston, when she gets off the plane and I can finally see her is always startling to me. I am sure it is in part because of her stability, her quiet calm presence so contrasting my own. But it is also because I never entirely feel whole when they are away. It is as if when they come back and our orbits converge, it is my moment of equilibrium, however brief.

When my children were young, I frequently had dreams of losing them, forgetting them in stores or in parks, and scrambling to find them, of them drowning in swimming pools. Panic was never as deep or biting as that.

When my children were little, I always knew where they were moving through the room around me. Interestingly, this same sort of shadow dance goes on now between my oldest daughter and me. I am aware of her movement around me like shadows moving on the canyon wall. I am conscious of her as she walks around the room, bouncing her baby against her chest, her pulse, her heartbeat a comfort to Aspen in strange settings. As she becomes a mother, I have reverted to sensing her as a child.

When Liffy first called me from college to tell me she was pregnant, I already knew. I had been thinking about it for weeks during the night. Even so when she called me late and we first talked about what it meant for us, one of the first thoughts that raced through my head was, "But I haven't taught her yet everything she needs to know. It's too soon." That night those thoughts ran through my head—how to be patient when you're bone tired, the importance of quiet in your life, of tasting the world outside this place, not to be afraid of anything.

During a Relief Society lesson on ancestry, my friend Nancy Miller showed a scrapbook of her family that included portraits of her and her husband, her parents, her grandparents, and their parents standing together as couples. It was stunning that hers was a legacy of couples, strong, loyal, and enduring. What made it stunning was my realization that what I handed my daughter was a legacy of single mothers, of women who often stand alone.

It was one of the greatest privileges of my life to share my granddaughter Aspen's birth. We spent the first six hours of Liffy's twenty-four-hour labor watching videos at home, soap operas, doing our first stage breathing in the comfort of a familiar place—my bedroom, the same bed where she had watched cartoons on Saturday mornings, the same bed we sat on as we talked about boys and difficult friends, her hopes and dreams. So it was a fitting place to begin this great adventure. By the time we went to the delivery ward of the University of Utah hospital, Liffy was in real pain (good pain as our birthing instructor told us). Nevertheless, the clerk at the desk asked us why we were there.

We looked at each other in exasperation at the absurdity of the question, and I said quietly, "My daughter is going to have a baby." Because all their rooms were full, they located us out in the lobby with a group of about twenty of the most obnoxious, loud-speaking, joking relatives of some woman in pain about twenty feet away. We laughed at the absurdity of our roommates in the hospital waiting room, the fact that we were stuck watching the *Munsters* with them until a delivery room was vacated.

Besides having an uncontrollable urge to eat Snickers bars, my head spun with reflections on birthing a baby, the striking remembrance that "labor," or travail as Laurel Ulrich reminds us in *Good Wives,* is work, remarkably difficult and painful work, that tries heavy muscles and threatens to leave us unable to breath or move. As Liffy moved through her labor and particularly the last most intense four hours, we worked together. I have few times in my life felt so connected to another human being. When she moved through a contraction, my own muscles tensed and I massaged her back, her legs and arms, neck and shoulders, and I whispered in her ear, "You're wonderful. You're almost there. You're doing great. Aspen is almost here."

This supportive work was incredibly difficult, complicated because what I really felt like doing was yelling out to anyone walking down the hall, particularly the young nurses and residents who were out there joking around, flirting, and passing time, "Come in here and stop my daughter's pain!" But I was also very aware she needed me to be calm, to be consistent and supportive, not to dissolve in anger, frustration, or tears.

I gave birth to six children, so I am no stranger to childbirth. But nevertheless, when I sat on the edge of her bed and held her bent-up left leg with my arm, her nurse holding the other, and watched the head of my first grandchild ease its way out, I was speechless. I have never seen anything so exquisitely beautiful or miraculous or amazing. Committed to letting the baby squeeze out without an episiotomy, the student doctor who delivered her (who looked as though he were about fifteen years old) let Aspen's head ooze out, and I remembered the birth of puppies, of kittens that I had observed as a girl, and had the same sweeping awe that the miracle of birth inspires. Despite all the mess of blood and fluids, the sterile equipment and gear, it all cleared away as this most amazing girl baby joined Liffy and me in our circle.

I had the most remarkable experience during those ten minutes that her head squeezed through. I felt the tangible, palpable presence of a woman I study, Zina Diantha Young, herself a midwife, present at the birth of her granddaughter, another Zina. Important to me was the warmth of the feeling, that I am sure came from her, that this was the most important miracle I might ever witness and that everything would be okay. That my daughter would be able to handle what this baby would bring to her and that their lives, and my own, would be better for the experience. I needed that comfort. And I believe that Zina brought it to me.

This was a remarkable opportunity to watch my daughter change from a girl into a mother, a woman. I marked her strength of character, her limitless joy and enthusiasm. The connection between them that is primal, physiological, social. Aspen lights up when Liffy enters the room, leans towards her as though pulled by some magnetic force. Here I remember the connection that we forget as they age and that begins sometimes to annoy us, challenge us.

It was little more than a month after Aspen's birth that my sixteen-year-old daughter, Emily, flew into the family room and plopped herself down on a chair across from me. It was her way to come to me like this, full of the day's events, stories about the crazy things that happened at school or how tired she was of work or whatever filled her head. This day, as she threw herself down, it was with genuine fatigue. It was written on her face, pale and blotchy. And I knew immediately that it was likely she too was pregnant.

My initial reaction was disbelief. How could she be so stupid? I had been thorough, even pushy, informing her on birth control, providing endless advice on how to avoid this type of trouble. How could this happen to me? (Again!) I was angry that she would do this to our family, to her sister Katelyn already strained by the difficulties of the year's changes. I saw this pain written on her dear face as a problem, one too many, that threatened to knock me to my knees.

Instead, one week now after the birth of yet another granddaughter, my perception has changed. I see this experience not as a problem (narcissistically my problem) but as a great teacher, a refiner, my daughter not as a problem child but my new hero.

It is perhaps ironic that for years we opened our home to unwed mothers. We were lucky enough to have a large, suburban home with far too many rooms for us to use, and we felt compelled to share our blessings with others. A series of these girls stayed with us for about ten years, for periods that ranged between six and eighteen months. We also cared for a few foster babies who were waiting for adoptive homes.

Although I don't necessarily buy notions about predestination, these relationships prepared me for what needed to be done with my own daughters. I toyed briefly (perhaps one black day) with sending Emily away for the duration of her pregnancy, perhaps to save face— for her?—for Katelyn—for me? But the idea appalled me. I had seen how those girls suffered through their pregnancies, their childbirths without their mothers and families. I had always said, never believing it would, "If this ever happened to me, I would keep my daughter home with me." And that is what we did.

In some ways Emily was better suited for pregnancy than her older sister, who moaned and groaned her way through months of nausea and bloat. Emily flourished. Her face regained the healthy glow it had when she was younger. Her golden hair shined and grew healthy and long. She took the earrings out of her nose, her eyebrow, and became obsessive about eating healthy foods, existing only in air free of pollutants, developing good habits. She laughed herself through those months, holding her chin up high when her friends, our neighbors, strangers gave her funny looks. She taught me about courage, self-respect.

It is astonishing how cruel adults can be to teenagers who struggle. Emily was, for example, lectured by a woman at the one-hour photo booth who thought Em's pregnant profile shots were disgusting. Regardless, determined to make her baby proud, Emily graduated from high school a year early, got terrific grades all year. It was so interesting to watch our middle child, hopelessly branded through life as difficult, challenging, spirited, jump rank and become a model of strength that her three older siblings looked to and admired for her courage.

It seemed she had reclaimed her life. She matured before our eyes. Even so, it was Emily's very difficult decision to place the baby up for adoption, knowing in her heart it would be the best gift she could give her. She read probably fifty different family portfolios before she selected a family who would do an open adoption with her.

Her birth, long anticipated as a potentially tragic occasion, was joyous; again the mood, the spirit, was set by Emily. This time Liffy and I stood on each side of Emily, holding her bent legs as she pushed Siera Jane out and into life. The tears rolled down our cheeks, but we laughed and cheered her on. A very different mood, it felt like a party really, a birthday party. A reminder once again that birth, regardless of the circumstances, is not a problem but a part of life to be cherished and learned from.

The ceremony when Emily gave her baby, her great gift to the adoptive parents—Wes and Carol Beckham—was, in my mind, brutal, a painful ripping away of the one thing that had brought my daughter, my own baby, her greatest joy. The expression of grief on her face haunts me and will always represent to me the greatest suffering I have personally witnessed. She knew she had her sisters, her brothers, me, and her father with her, but even still it was her decision, her sorrow, her future. Thirteen-year-old Katelyn wrote her a sweet expression of caring that night. "I used to think you were the most selfish person in our family, but now I know you are not. You loved your baby more than you loved yourself. You would rather she be happy than you. I love you." We all learned about love from the birth of this baby. And now our family circle includes the Beckhams, Wes and Carol, who waited fifteen years for their baby daughter, now Kristen Siera, people like all of us who had benefitted from Emily's graceful efforts at mothering.

Perhaps twenty years ago I had an epiphany of sorts. I was a diligent student at the university and very serious about understanding the significance of my life. I went to our family cabin in Midway for a week away. I brought my sketch books, my Jose Feliciano and John Denver records, my scriptures, and other books. I spent the week in blissful solitary sketching, hiking, and listening to music in the beautiful woods. My last day I was restless because it seemed I hadn't found any particular answers. I had spent much of the week meditating, trying to see clearly where I needed to go next. I was very consciously asking God for these answers. I went on a hike late that final afternoon, higher on the mountain than before in the rich autumn colors.

On my descent I was quite tired but so excited by the day that I started to run down the path. I ran past a flock of sheep grazing in a quiet grove of aspen trees. I felt as though I was dancing down the hill when I tripped coming around a curve and literally sailed through the air down a sharp decline about forty feet before I landed. I was dazed, bruised, and bloody, and immediately scared. The fact that no one knew where I was, whether I had been hiking or where, flashed through my head. My independence, which had moments before been exhilarating, seemed to make me most vulnerable. I remember crying out a prayer, "Help me!" Looking up the sharp rocky hill I would have to climb to get back on the path, I was terrified, and again and again I said, "Please help me. I will do anything when I get back. Please just help me." And when I tried to stand, it seemed my ankle had been sprained or something, it certainly hurt. And I literally had to pull myself up that hill, inch by inch, smearing mud and leaves and rocks all over my chest and legs. It seemed like hours before I reached the top, and I got there purely by will power. When I finally pulled myself over the rocky edge, brilliant sunlight beamed through the aspen leaves above me and it seemed (and this is my epiphany) that everything would be all right, that I would be safe. As I stood up and brushed the debris off my legs, feeling that sunlight on my back and thinking nothing had ever felt so good, I was flooded with the feeling (and maybe it was God who put this feeling in me) that it was me who pulled me out of that mess, that it was my strength and determination that had pulled me up that hill. That realization of personal power was perhaps the most important thing I learned that year, and finally, after almost twenty-five years, I have felt it again.

The experiences of life that threaten to destroy us become our greatest teachers. Sometimes we are faced with decisions that have the potential of breaking us. But we must face them with courage rather than fear. With hope rather than dread. We must trust in our selves and our futures. We must live as if our dreams have been fulfilled.

Aspen, Kristen Siera, Liffy, Rachael, Emily, Katelyn, my sons Jason and Patrick, all have taught me about the miracle of life in all its richness. The circle forged by love and experiences—good and bad—that have formed our days have provided me with the greatest opportunity for growth. Being a mother is how I define myself. It has been the greatest gift. I carry that model into my classrooms, into my relationships with others, into my exploration for a greater understanding of myself.

For mothering is above all else about caring and respect.

My grandmother once told me, "Never forget who you are." I have tried to remember. I had forgotten the lesson I learned in the sunshine on that mountainside. I have found that there is a spiritual basis to attention, to self-reflection, a humility required of us in waiting upon the emergence of pattern from experience. In any experience other moments are present, and so they are with me. When I write about my life at forty-five years old, I am accompanied by a teenager and a girl of ten who stared out the window wondering how she could shape her life. I am accompanied by a strong-boned woman raised by pioneers, Mormon born and bred, belief and devotion in her blood. I am accompanied by a small woman, whose heart opens to every weak person who comes along, who gives them what she should have gotten from others. I am privileged to stand next to a new mother, still a child herself who has shown the greatest love and maturity, my teacher. I stand in the circle with four strong golden young women, with my mother, her mother.

It is as if I move in the experiences of the past year through a dusty Mormon town in southern Utah to a suburban neighborhood at the base of Mt. Olympus. We stand on a plateau looking out on the red rock of a canyon, we join in my office bedroom, in my daughters' birthing room. We are together, my mother, my grandmother, and me, Aspen, Kristen Siera, and my four daughters—Elizabeth, Rachael, Emily, and Katelyn. Their story is my story. My story is their story. Our lives form a circle.

Insight comes from setting our experiences side by side, learning to let them speak to one another. This, then, is how I have gone about remembering, so that my children will remember too. I like best an explanation of mothering as one standing by with a safety net spread beneath the feet of my children who play in the air above me. I hope they will not view my presence with dismay, but will let it help them rise as high as they choose, secure in the knowledge of my support. It is frightening to consider that pulling the net too tightly might send them bouncing off into space or, leaving the grip too loose, letting them crash to the ground.

What I really want most is for my children to be able to soar confidently in their own sky, wherever that might be, to be the pilots of their own plane, agents in their own lives. And if there is space for me alongside them, then I will have, indeed, reaped what I have attempted to sow.

As women, the lines, the threads of strength, pride, courage, and beauty run through us, not around us. Tangible as rope but fine as silk, these connections are magnified by the experience of mothering. I didn't need to worry about teaching my daughter how to mother, it runs through her blood. It is a part of her memory. As I write this, I am recovering from a hysterectomy and mourn the loss of my uterus, my ability to give birth. I remember, at my granddaughter's birth, they asked my daughter if she wanted to see the placenta and we both were a little disgusted by the prospect. But I wish that I could have seen my uterus. It was the source of the greatest joy I have felt, the incubator of the finest human beings I have been privileged to know. And as I move into a new part of my life, I mark its passing, one of the best parts of me is gone.

Once again, as I lie in my four-poster bed, this time sunshine dancing in the window warming my arms and face, I wish for a sister with whom I could share this change. She would rub my back or perhaps brush my hair, and remind me that she understands and that we will share new things that will surprise us with their richness. Instead I have daughters. Emily who makes me a special dinner (oriental chicken salad, my favorite); Rachael who calls after a long day at work the distance from Boston in the middle of the night to get a recipe for tortillas and to chat; Katelyn who stills bursts through the door after a day of school with all the energy and happiness imaginable; and Liffy my dreamer, another mother, daughter still, friend and partner in joy and sorrow. My sisters, my daughters.

A Circle of Women

Elizabeth Bradley

I WATCHED MY YOUNGER SISTER, Emily, give her child to another woman. She was seventeen and wanted her daughter to have a family with a mom and dad. Her long-gone boyfriend denied being the father, and Emily knew her child deserved more. At an age when most teenagers are having the time of their life, she was making the decision of her life. A decision she will remember, at times question, but in her heart know she did the right thing.

There is no easy way to look for a family to adopt your child. So many requirements. If they are not perfect, they will not do. I watched from the sidelines, voicing an opinion I know my sister at times listened to.

Emily stumbled upon a family in Texas, Carol and Wes and their son Bryce. Bryce was adopted five years ago. Emily met Bryce's birth mother at her counseling group. Emily knew in her heart that this Texas family was going to raise her daughter. Bryce wanted a little sister.

Exactly one week after I had my own daughter, Emily became pregnant. Had she not seen me? Had I not shown her how alone being alone can be? Why had she been so careless? Why had I?

I am supposed to protect my sisters. Ease them into this world, as she did her daughter. I should have warned her that boys do not stick around, men do, perhaps. Love is confused with lust, and with lust there is not responsibility. Why did I not prevent her pain from happening? I should have known, but I was blinded, distracted by my own pregnancy, problems, life. She was crying out for help in the only way she knew how.

Tracy Chapman's voice played quietly, whispering words for Emily in the final moments before sharing her daughter: "If you'll wait for me, I'll come for you." Emily will always be there.

Emily needs time to grow up herself, although watching the way she handled herself through this experience, I know she has grown up. She is no longer a girl, but a woman, a mother. Her child is in another state, but part of Emily is there too. It is an open adoption. Emily can call anytime. They send pictures. They want Emily to be a part of her daughter's life. But that part is limited.

Sometimes Emily calls me in the middle of the night, longing for that missing part, the cry, the warmth of the innocent breath. I talk to her, trying to comfort her in the only way I know how. Her voice is distant, and perhaps mine is too. We need each other.

Emily has told me often that I influenced her in her decision to give Kristen Siera a family with both a father and a mother. She has watched me as a single mother and seen the struggles I have faced. I never know how to reply. She is right, it is hard.

My cousin Jake is adopted. His birth mother handed him over to my aunt Shauna. She was young and wanted more for her newborn son, a family with a mother and a father.

My aunt Shauna is a social worker. One day she was speaking to a young woman who resembled her son Jake. Could she be his birth mother? Shauna never saw any pictures or never knew her name. Jake's mother, Ann, sat on the other side of Shauna's desk that afternoon. Fifteen years after the transition from mother to mother was made, these two women came together. Shauna and Ann sat in the office and cried. So many questions were answered for both women.

The adoption agency was on the second floor in a modest corner office. Both families sat in the room. Strangers sharing a child. A connection for life forming. Two families coming together through the life of a child.

The smile on the faces of those Texans burns an image in my heart. During labor my mother and I held Emily's hands, a circle of women. I found myself pushing with my sister, feeling the birth of her child. She was so calm. Emily passed her child into the arms of a woman who was denied the miracle of birth.

I want to share Emily's pain as a woman shares her child.

Children

All Parts of Myself

Karen Farb

I AM THE MOTHER OF A three-year-old. He is, I suspect, like most three-year-old boys—past the physical capacities of the toddler years, yet still a bit entrenched in the two-year-old Dr. Jekyll and Mr. Hyde. Sweet songs, hugs and kisses sprinkled with curiosity, new words, bursts of energy, small discoveries for hours, then seemingly from nowhere, the tyrant rears his power through kicks, hits, spits: everything aimed at me. He is exquisite in living: passionate about chocolate, "softs," his binky, snacks, *his* small table, sleeping, hiding, scary noises, and the mystery of Bambi's mother. As a baby, he was joyous, reveled in breastfeeding, loved to be snuggled, held—yet always quite adamant about trying to stand—even at just a few weeks.

I am sure the first year of his life was the best year of my life. He was a big, bouncy, fat baby. "Tangible joy was felt," said a friend as she described visiting me in the hospital. Just a few hours old, he would look around the room and put his arm over his eyes, too bright. And I would lift him with burning pain at my stitches and look at this beautiful life, fragile with its newness. I held his body, *him*, this new person. This was familiar, the joy, the wonder. I'd done this before. Someone else I held, another baby captured my heart with a surprise sweep of love, simultaneous joy and burning pain. Both present and past, inseparable these lives from me and yet each distinct, different.

I had a baby girl. She too shied away from lights. She preferred my skin to the blankets she was wrapped in, though I was afraid to unwrap her. Her birth was much less complicated than his. I lay in the hospital with her on me, not wanting to move for fear of missing a second of feeling her, being with her, and the joy and the pain that lay there with us. Still, like a photograph, I remember wanting to hold that feeling. But I moved, I moved and the connection was severed.

I was a freshman at Brigham Young University. I had all the world to look forward to: I overpacked my small dorm room, taught Relief Society in my ward, and I found that I loved my humanities classes despite the "can't get a job with that degree" counsel from my parents. I had a sizable interest in boys. I moved out of the dorms for spring term and found myself in a very controlling relationship. I was young and didn't really think the situation was threatening—I studied, went dancing, went to movies. And then I was date raped.

At the time nobody at BYU was talking about date rape. I thought rape was something that happened at the blade of a stranger's knife. With nowhere to turn, I turned against myself. This is what I was taught to do: I was the woman, I was to blame, I was guilty. The only recourse was to go to the bishop. Unfortunately the man got to him first. When it came my turn to go in, I wasn't asked what happened, I was disfellowshipped. Looking back, I was so unsure about what had happened myself that I wonder if I could have even described to the bishop my unwillingness, my fear. I thought every sexual encounter with someone you know was supposed to be a desired one.

I thought the incident was over. I was disfellowshipped: I could repent and get back on track. The weeks passed and spring finals were approaching and I found myself unable to eat anything but baked potatoes until about 4:00 in the afternoon. My period hadn't started yet—though I wasn't worried since this was often the case. But somewhere I knew. Some place inside of me I knew that the worst thing had happened to me: I was pregnant but could not acknowledge that it might be true. This went on for days until finally I walked into the hospital during their Thursday free testing hours. The sight of the needle puncturing my skin made me throw up.

I was driving to Salt Lake City to have dinner with a friend that afternoon when we pulled over off the freeway and called from a pay phone to check for the test results. I wasn't able to stand at the phone and call with the desert heat swelling up in my stomach, so my friend dialed. I remember sitting in her passenger seat, door wide open in the dry wind of June, listening to her ask for my test results. All I remember was her question into the phone: "Could you please check those results again?" The question swept through me throwing my head back, screaming towards the heavens.

Somehow word got out. My bishop called me and I went in, again following the man who had done this to me. This time, again without any questions, I was counseled to marry. I looked around the room and with all of the strength I could muster, I said I will not make two mistakes out of one. I will not let this event determine the rest of my life. Those words now haunt me. I was naive to think that this event would not affect the rest of my life.

A few memories of that period of my life are particularly strong. I remember the desperation—desperation I had never known before that and have rarely felt since. Desperation to turn back the clock, to have time stop—stop long enough for me to think. But time doesn't stop, and pregnancies grow larger with time, despite my prayers to God to make this go away, to miscarry. The only way I could make it all stop was to put it out of my mind. I worked very hard at acting like it wasn't real—despite my changing body, growing belly. I separated my mind from my body. And so I continued to work, socialize, go to singles' wards with my clothes tightening across my stomach. Time was crushing me—crushing my insides, crushing my life.

I finally broke down and was silently whisked away by my parents and bishop to another home of a bishop far enough away. But I have never known such loneliness, such desperation, such remorse, regret, self-hatred. I punished myself daily for ever getting involved with this man. I punished myself for doing something, everything wrong. The world was no longer a place where I could be an agent. The only control I could get was through my self-punishment. Perhaps *then* all would be better. The baby was my penitence, and as soon as it was birthed I would be forgiven and go back to my normal life. My bishop confirmed my self-punishment by decreeing that only after the birth could I take the sacrament again.

I told my social worker at LDS Social Services that I felt like a surrogate mother. She said that this was a good sign, that it meant I was dealing with this well. She wasn't concerned when I explained that I wasn't doing so well—that I just had to wait for my body to get through this pregnancy. She didn't mention that I might be repressing my feelings, that you can't just separate your mind from your body and that some day all of this would blow up in my face. She also didn't prepare me for the life stopping emotions of motherhood and the ambivalence

I might feel at the thought of giving my baby up. She just cheered me on with discussions about what type of parents I would want for my child, how my baby would be going to a good LDS home, and what I could do after the baby was born. And these were things that I did want to talk about. I so longed to be at college with my friends, taking classes, doing the things that a nineteen-year-old does.

I was working hard to continue both my education (I dyed my hair and took night classes at a local university) as well as my spiritual growth. And I felt very spiritual. I didn't question my bishop's notion that I could take the sacrament again—be forgiven—only after the birth. I came to realize that I felt that I, as a pregnant woman, was unworthy, and so was the baby. I couldn't tell anyone the truth. With dyed hair, fake glasses, a cubic zirconium on my ring finger, I told everyone at school that I was married to a man who had a lot of business in Argentina. I had letters with air-mail stamps to prove it as I continued my correspondence with a few missionaries in South America. I was just house-sitting for a year. Even my siblings believed the story.

Soon before the birth I could no longer put off what was happening—both physically and emotionally. I was big, with a big hiccuping baby inside, and I loved this little ball that so obviously stuck out of me. Her birth was beautiful. I paced the hospital corridors at night, utterly confused by my feelings. I thought that her birth would be my delivery from purgatory. Instead it felt like a rock was crushing me. I loved this baby, my daughter. She was peaceful and had a beautiful little nose. Her gentle, warm little body just fit into my arms. I was being crushed by the weight of what I felt like I had to do. I had to get on with my life, yet my life was also cradled in my arms. How could I both care for a child and go on with my life? The two seemed absolutely opposed. No one had talked to me about the possibility of keeping her save one friend. She was the only one that suggested that I could keep this dear baby.

I walked out of the hospital doors alone, not understanding what I had given up nor what an effect this had on me. I mourned for days. It rained outside and the ocean down the hill was black. I left my window open and the water flooded the sill, warping the wood. I was completely overtaken by grief. Heartache filled my stomach, physically sweeping through me like ocean swells, currents of remorse. Grief and confusion exhausted my worn body and mind. I went back to school and believed whole-heartedly that life was linear—that we go from one event to another, each event discrete and separate from another. Within a year I fell in love with someone who also was interested in travel, schooling, arts, and I married him and found the stability and the life I thought I needed. I didn't think that my marriage and my repugnancy towards my past had anything to do with the date rape and adoption.

I went on, lived abroad, moved to new exciting cities. While traveling through Europe, a friend we had just met reported to be a clairvoyant, looked me in the eye and told me that I should forget about what troubling thing had happened to me in the past. I was shocked—how could she know?—I thought I had forgotten about it. Was my behavior revealing something I thought was not a part of my life anymore? Returning to the states, my husband started graduate school. I worked hard to put him through school and when he was nearly done with his degree, I applied to school. I was accepted into a fairly prestigious graduate program, which surprised even me. I spent the week sharing the news with family and friends that I was going back to school. I was making a skirt for myself and found my waist had grown an inch in a week. I knew it. Again I lost control of my life. My period was late, and though I knew, I tried to think nothing of it—this irregularity had certainly happened before. I ignored my body. I could not talk about the possibility of pregnancy. At 5:55 a.m. on a spring day, I found out I was pregnant for the second time, and went screaming into the bedroom.

For all the hell my pregnancies were, I must say that the children I have birthed have given me indescribable joy. The joy and the pain live together inside of me. My time with my first child was very short—I was a mother to her in the womb, during her birth, and for a few very short days thereafter. I know that mothering is much more than pregnancy, birth, and a stay in the hospital. And yet mothering does start with time shared between two people in one body, a split of that relationship, birthing into a new one. And then a long relationship, built and negotiated between two separate beings. Through my wondrous and joyous relationship with my son, I have learned what I have lost with my daughter. Now that I know what mothering is, what a child is, I have finally been able to grieve my loss of my daughter. This has been torture because she isn't completely lost, she is out there somewhere. And now

I think that I *am* enough for her. I am a mommy and how I wish I could be her mommy too.

Though this essay is about motherhood—it is about my whole life. Motherhood does not just happen *in* a woman's life, it happens *to* a woman's life, fundamentally altering it forever. Although I have many other things that define my life, my work, my interests, my motherhood is what shapes all other decisions. Perhaps the idea of determining our lives is a myth that ignores the realities of birth, of caring for another, of mothering in its many forms. Every day I balance how much time to spend with my son and how much time to spend on my studies. I revisit my decisions constantly, checking which worked and which didn't. This constant reconsideration does drive me a bit up the wall. How nice it would be to just decide that I am going to raise my child with a prescribed set of gender ideas or life ideals. Or that I am going to spend this much time with my son every day or this much time away from him. But I suppose I feel that I have already lost a child and a part of myself once—and so now I am working to make sure that I keep both my child and myself.

This is tricky—to keep an eye on not losing myself. I was taught by example that a woman is to sacrifice herself for her family. It is easy to fall back on—I know how to do it. But I don't think such mothering is necessary or beneficial. While I was cared for and loved, I never knew my mother as a person: her interests, her likes and dislikes, what her needs were. She rarely did anything for herself. She let her children and her husband determine her life. And so for myself as well as for my child, I am trying to balance his needs with my own. And I am going back, reaching back to find who I was as a girl. Going back and trying to embrace the girl who was sure of herself, that understood she should trust herself. Back when I understood that we are all fundamentally spiritual beings and so we should value listening to the authority of our own voice. I have valued the authority of others—church authority, academic journals, parents, professors. And now I have been working towards finding and listening to my voice.

Taking an active role in constructing my life means really listening to myself, and acknowledging all parts of myself—even the parts I didn't want to acknowledge. It also means listening to those around me and understanding what I want, what my child wants and negotiating this with my family and with God. I think we are accustomed to finding a path and passively going down it—no further need for questioning, for doubt, for self-appraisal. Life and relationships require constant questioning and checking. It is constant work—figuring where I am, where others are around me, and where it is I am and we are headed.

But isn't this motherhood? The constant work of checking and questioning where I am, where my child is, whether it be a physical place, or a psychological or emotional one. And then appraising where it is that I as a parent am, and trusting where I should go or negotiate with my son—us, the relationship of mother-child—to go from there. This is motherhood. Being open to all parts of myself, my child, others—being open to past and to possibilities, to both joy and pain. Allowing myself to feel and know the contradictions and allowing my child to slowly learn the complexities of emotion, reality, choice. I'm allowing the distant experiences of my life to come up to the surface and color my thoughts, my feelings, my actions, my relationships—like a palette, changing, mixing, unfolding. The present is never without past. The double-vision is not double-vision after all, but a kaleidoscope of color, pattern, and emotion alive and unfolding within.

Mary and Martha

Marni Asplund-Campbell

I watch her face in the fading room,
how her eyes flick to the window,
aware of strangers, and comprehend
the dishes on the table, with crusts of cereal
along their rims, sticky cups, the butter
melting between us. We can smell
the bathwater growing cold, the dull edge
of tub soap quickly hardening.
Crumbs stick to our elbows,
and a thin line of ants streams across the floor,
past rubber bands and legos, and our bare feet.
We sit for hours, just like this, talking
and waiting for some answers,
abandoned as we are by daylight.

And you, my Lord, are the child
sleeping in my bed,
your breath sweet
with the day's milk,
your eyes dusted
with salt from the tears
I let you cry
all alone in the dark room.
You upbraid me
with your sorrow,
and I can only offer
a warm embrace
as penitence,
holding you closely
to my tired, tired heart.

Poetry

Lara Candland

EMANUELLE PUTS CARROTS through a strainer. The baby's mouth opens wide. After he eats his bowl of carrots, Emanuelle puts him to her breast. The milk comes out fast. This makes her sleepy and she lies on the couch with Nicky and they both fall asleep.

Emanuelle hears music. While she sleeps, there is a soundtrack … but what she really wants is poetry. The poetry runs hard as sap … she is moving across the bay. She sees water and light and she remembers the verses all wrong … when I think how I used my light … when I think how my light is spent … Nicky stirs and Emanuelle thinks how she should get up and put the chicken in a pan. Nicky doesn't cry much and Jack isn't picky about dinner. She will just sprinkle some things on the chicken and stick it in the oven. She might clean the floor.

The line she is searching for does not come. She does not fall asleep.

Emanuelle gets down on the floor and scrubs. Nicky still sleeps. His blood is thick like mine, his mother thinks, thick and slow, he likes to sleep, he has too much phlegm, he was born under Saturn. But these things are not all bad. The house smells like soap and chicken. Nicky is always happy.

"Are you a minimalist?" Jack says when he reads her poetry. Emanuelle does not answer. My blood is thick, I am indecisive, she thinks, I am like Hamlet, my message is one of despair … When in disgrace with fortune and men's eyes … she likes to write poetry because it is short. The message is usually one of despair. My blood runs thick, cold, hard as sap, like poems, she thinks. She writes her stuff fast but it comes hard: it boils for a long time and torments her and tears her apart. Then she writes fast. A lot of times she forgets her great lines.

When Jack gets home, he will like the smell of soap and chicken.

Nicky will arise from his nap and be all warm and soft and sweet, smelling of his mother's milk.

Those lines on paper, the great ones, are rare, or non-existent.

"This is depressing," Jack says, "you're always so depressed." This is what he says when he reads his wife's poetry. "But I like it," he adds.

Jack will quote lines she is unfamiliar with—thou art summoned by sickness, Death's herald and champion. They are manly lines, I go back to Korea. Do I ever.

"I like your feet a lot," Jack says, "a lot." He touches them. Emanuelle soaks them in water and soap. She rubs them with oil.

"Emanuelle," Jack says, "where's this from: It was not a very white jacket, but white enough ..."

"Are you asking me because you want to know, or is this a test?"

"Test," Jack says. They are eating little cups of pudding in bed.

"Melville," she says. They are living in New York now. Soon they will be living in Boston. Emanuelle feeds Jack spoonfuls of pudding. They are watching t.v. A man is wearing all black and pretending to be German. He is making fun of Germans.

They turn off the set and they hear sirens and people using fireworks. They hear a car stereo. Nicky's little bed is in the front room and Ellie gets up to feed him.

Emanuelle checks the mirror on her way back to bed. She says prayers. She snuggles up to Jack and falls asleep. Jack gets up early. He never cares how much sleep he gets. Ellie does not like waking up to an empty bed. When Nicky awakens, she puts him in bed with her and feeds him. Then they both fall asleep. Then Emanuelle usually dreams of Jack. When she wakes up, she calls him on the phone. By night on my bed I sought him whom my soul loveth: I sought him but I found him not, she says to Jack over the phone.

Emanuelle puts in a load of laundry and hangs all the colors out to dry on the fire escape. She takes Nicky to the park. They watch some boys playing basketball. When Nicky was first born, Emanuelle thought she was skinny again. Now she thinks she is fat. She does not like her reflection in the windows. In the park they sit on a bench and drink juice. A woman pinches Nicky's cheek. "He's lovely," she says. "You should try olive oil on that," she says, pointing to a little rash on Nicky's cheek. Emanuelle has long hair. She holds it back with her hand while she speaks to the woman. She offers the woman her bagel because it seems that she is hungry. Nicky laughs at her and she touches his face again.

"My name is Miriam," the woman says.

"I am Emanuelle."

"This is a very nice name," Miriam says. "Your mother has good taste."

Miriam eats the bagel. Emanuelle offers her a banana and that is all the food she has with her. Miriam eats the banana. They walk on Broadway to 110th Street. They stop in a shop and have falafel and coffee. Miriam seems sleepy.

At Emanuelle's apartment, while Miriam sleeps, Emanuelle cleans her oven. Nicky sits in his basket on the floor next to his mother. Miriam is wearing Emanuelle's nightie. Emanuelle scrubs the bathtub. She does not want Miriam to think she is a bad housekeeper. When the kitchen and bathroom are spotless, she organizes her desk and writes a note to her sister. She turns some very quiet music on the stereo and feeds Nicky. Nicky cries after he eats. His mother changes his diaper and pats his back until he burps. Where did you find that little tear? I found it waiting when I got here. What makes your forehead so smooth and high? A soft hand stroked it as I went by. Nicky and his mother nap on the couch. Emanuelle dreams of the water again, a harbor that is not Boston, a plane headed west, a sun she has never seen in New York.

While Emanuelle sleeps, Miriam is in the kitchen chopping vegetables. When she wakes up, Miriam says, "If you run out for a little meat, I can make something delicious." So they go down to the butcher's and pick up some beef. They buy a parsnip at the grocery store at Miriam's request. When they return, they smell onions cooking. Miriam throws the beef into the pot and adds vegetables and paprika. Emanuelle opens a bottle of wine.

When it was not raining, a low mist moved across the paddies, blending the elements into a single gray element, and the war was cold and pasty and rotten. Jack said this to Emanuelle shortly after they first met. She had not been able to place it. She is too embarrassed to ask Jack where it came from now. Miriam's goulash simmers in the kitchen. Nicky and Miriam play on the couch. Your father went to work, Miriam sings, he will return. Nicky giggles. Emanuelle has given

Miriam a sheaf of poems. Miriam reads while she plays with Nicky. Emanuelle holds a book that she is not reading.

"You think it is," Miriam says, "but your message is essentially not one of despair." Emanuelle closes her book. "I'm right," Miriam says, "trust me."

Jack should be home soon. "It was a bad time," he once said. And it was. It had been a bad time then. "Who said this?" Jack said once, "The heart does not choose who it loves. ..." Emanuelle did not answer. Who chooses? she thought.

Miriam continues to leaf through the poems. Emanuelle stands by the window, waiting for Jack to come out of the subway. It is getting dark early now, and it rains lightly. Emanuelle bounces Nicky on her hip. Miriam reads and reads. Jack does not appear as Emanuelle waits by the window. Saw ye him whom my soul loveth? Nicky falls asleep on his mother's shoulder ... there is a moon out already. The moon in its flight ... Emanuelle thinks. She is tired of waiting. As she turns from the window, the moon, evanescent, fades behind a cloud. I'd prefer not to think it was beauty on the wane.

Speech Therapy

Karin England

THE YEARS IN WHICH OUR SON Porter should have been ac-
quiring language were pretty rough for all of us. I think Mark's mother
still attributes Porter's speech disorder to the turmoil of those years. As
much as I want to resist this theory, I can't imagine the circumstances
of those years were any help.

He started and then stopped talking within, maybe, a month.
Started right on schedule, eighteen months old, just like the older two.
He said, moving his lips with a motor boat sound, "Bpp—Bpp," for
"root beer," and "Ha—Pa," for "Grandpa," my dad. Two favorites, associated, reasonably, together.

Then he stopped, completely, for the next year and a half. It wasn't
that Porter didn't vocalize, and it wasn't that he sounded particularly
weird. He just didn't make words. He made sounds. Waved his arms,
danced his fingers, caricatured his expressions like a wide-eyed mime.
I concentrated on not worrying as long as it seemed it wasn't affecting
him emotionally. I ran through a list of nieces and nephews who talked
a little late, or idiosyncratically, on Mark's side of the family. They had
just seemed to need a little extra time. I refused to consider my cousin
Janet.

Mark and I both grew up in a conservative religion. We've embraced and fought it in different ways. Although he's trying to hang in
and I'm doing my best to bail, we aren't too far apart when it comes to
bottom-line values. We've made a conscious effort to put aside, as best
we can, the rigid gender biases of Mormonism, for example. Mark is an
artist. He works at home. I teach English at a large local state college.
Once our son Christian said, "Mom, it's so weird. Josh's dad goes to
work." Still, I was the one who was raised to expect to be the primary
childkeeper. Although I spend as many hours with the children as

Mark does, I'm the one who tends to accrue the guilt. He grew up out-side the intimate circle of child care. It's more difficult for him to main-tain an instinctive focus on parenting. Sometimes we lose sight of each other, sometimes we just get too damn close. It's hard to keep a clear vision in the heart of things.

Porter's eyes, blue-green prisms, flash with humor and animation. He and my father trade mischievous smirks at family events. Some-thing inside of him doesn't quite contain as he walks, rolls, hops, lunges, throws a rock, drives a toy truck. He just spills over, laps out over the edges. He jerks my arm when he holds my hand, writhes like a puppy when he's on my lap. Porter has four cowlicks: two at his fore-head, two at the back. Usually his hair sticks straight up at the conver-gence. His middle name is "Scout." Sometimes we call him "Scoutabout" or "Scooter."

He had invented so many hand signs for us by the time he was three and a half, that we invented one for his name, too. We held two fingers, like feathers, rising from the backs of our heads, like Indian scouts. Like we know anything about Indian scouts. By then we had sought help on the speaking problem and had been told that Porter had a "moderate" hearing impairment, moving toward "severe" at the lower frequencies.

"It's like he's hearing us from under the water," the audiologist ex-plained. "He can hear sounds, but the actual articulations are blurred."

I asked how it was that Porter understood us so clearly, and so invariably.

"He's obviously a very bright little boy," he answered. "He's just learned to compensate. He hears a consistent language from us. It just sounds different to him than it does to us. He's probably speaking the same sounds he hears. And he watches for visual signals when the lis-tening fails him."

We considered this. We watched him closely during the following weeks. Porter did make a lot of vocal sounds, always vowel-ish but with the dips and rises of English, and pretty much a familiar iambic rhythm. I experimented with his comprehension in different situations. I would speak to him directly, watching his eyes. Or I would say things side-ways, like, "Anybody want a popsicle?" to no one in particular. I would stand behind him and ask questions at different decibels.

"Porter, shall we go out and get the mail?"

"Scoot, would you bring me that little yellow car?"

"Porter, do you want to go play in the sandpile?"

He always responded appropriately.

I called to him from different rooms, varying distances. He always turned to me, or appeared from where he'd been. I tried sentences of varying length and complexity. He could follow long sequences of information. I was afraid that if it wasn't hearing, it would be something scarier. Some kind of aphasia, less explainable.

Porter would ask for candy with his hands close together, pinching his fingers and twisting in opposite directions as if he were opening a Tootsie Roll, his eyes lighting with anticipation. He would scoop his right hand, palm downward, dropping it diagonally and leveling to a stop to say he wanted to go play on his friend Hayden's slide. He walked two fingers and pointed in his intended direction to tell us where he wanted to go. He walked his fingers vertically to tell us he was tired: he was climbing the ladder to his bunk bed.

But directly representative signs and pantomimes, of course, have severe expressive limitations. They can only address the immediate, the concrete. The gap between Porter's comprehension and his expression was widening rapidly. It was beginning to affect his personality. We enrolled him in speech therapy while we were still trying to pin down the specific hearing problems. Our first session was discouraging. Porter tested capable of vocalizing only seven standard English phonemes, all vowels, mostly short. If it required any exertion or contact of lips, teeth, or tongue, Porter couldn't copy the sound.

The speech therapist was distressed. "Well, we might as well test his comprehension," she sighed. "Don't expect too much, though."

She was talking to me, Porter's mother.

She pulled out her wire-bound comprehension testing book. She said words, he pointed. She asked him questions, he signaled the responses. She kept turning pages.

"Actually, he seems to understand quite a bit," she conceded. She seemed to resent this.

We took Porter to Salt Lake City for batteries of hearing tests, culminating in a definitive consensus that, although there were slight and seasonal fluctuations in his hearing ability, actual hearing loss was minimal and did not account for his profound inability to speak.

We went back on possible causes.

My Aunt Elaine, Janet's mother, told me, "They thought it was hearing in Janet, too, at first." I stifled a shudder. Janet is five years younger than I am, looked perfectly normal as a small child, still does except for her odd gait and the incomprehensible expression on her face.

"What is it with Janet?" I asked, trying for a natural tone of voice. I have heard theories my whole life, one succeeding another, never enough to clear it up for me.

"We still don't know, exactly," Elaine said. Janet, as usual, had seated herself on the couch so close to me our hip bones ground against each other. Her face, dripping with oatmeal, hovered six inches from mine. Her hands went from my hair to her lap to my knees back to wringing themselves as I leaned around to speak to Elaine.

"Janet, come here. Come sit by me," Elaine coaxed. Janet stood up abruptly and plopped herself beside her mother.

"Whatever it is," Elaine said, "It happened at the very first cell divisions of the pregnancy. Whole parts of her brain just didn't form. It's pretty obvious in the scans. You don't have to be an expert to recognize it."

By the time Janet was three, it was clear to everyone that something was seriously wrong. It wasn't just that she didn't talk. As she grew, she had the strength of ten kids her age, truly, as if her inability to comprehend physical limitations literally freed her from them. She could climb anything, fast and vertical. She could reach in the crib and pull a baby out by the leg, flinging it over her head and across the room. All of us cousins were frightened of her. When she finally began to speak, she picked up phrases whole, like a demented tape recorder, and echoed them over and over. "It's my birthday. My birthday. It's my birthday, birthday, it's my birthday." "I got my hair cut. Look, I got my haircut. I got my hair cut." Her eyes gleamed, shrewd and feral. She would grab me by the sleeve. "I got my hair cut." Her voice bounced like a Hare Krishna dance.

When Janet was thirteen or fourteen, one therapist made an intriguing suggestion. She told Elaine that she believed Janet's intelligence was near normal, that Janet seemed to understand an awful lot of what was going on around her. She pegged Janet as a severe aphasic, whose only real problem was a profound inability to produce language; Janet took it in, but couldn't give it back. Her demented behavior might actually be due to the severe frustration of an intelligent mind incapable of communicating to the outside world.

That's the theory that stuck with me over the years. It terrified me. Janet and I are associated closely in the minds of many of my extended family. Elaine was my father's younger sister. Dad was the first in his large immediate family to have children. My sister Marti and I were the first two grandchildren, two little girls not much more than a year apart. We had three years of glory, spoiled rotten I'm sure, before cousins began to multiply.

Elaine's first two were little girls as well. Janet was the second, like me. Elaine always associated Jenny and Janet with Marti and me. The similarities and tragic differences came up repeatedly, especially as we grew older. Janet looks like me. Of sixty-three grandchildren, six of us girls took on a specific genetic pattern, not more than five-two, small-boned, thin, all, apparently, finished to the last structural detail like a great-grandmother we never met. Janet and I look eye-to-eye. Our hair is the same color and our fingers begin and end at the same points. She's lost some excess energy over the last few years. She still paces, wiggles, and fidgets, but doesn't scale walls. But she can dance, and I'm not much good at that. My gift is language, of which she has nearly none.

The brain damage information doesn't jive with the theory that Janet is merely aphasic. Still, it's the defining thing. I have no idea how much she actually comprehends. I read once, in junior high, a rather lurid book called *Unsolved Mysteries of the Universe,* or something. I read about the Bermuda Triangle, was introduced to Kaspar Hauser. I read something about a town in Germany where a single cloven track, most likely Satan's, had appeared in a perfect trail for miles through the new-fallen snow. The one that reminds me of Janet was the one about a man in India who, even with his eyes bandaged and cloth wrapped around his head, could see what was in front of him, could ride a bike through the streets of Calcutta with unerring vision.

If there was ever a kid who could comprehend on a normal linguistic level but not reciprocate, it was Porter. And he didn't climb walls like a fly or snatch babies from their beds. He wasn't uncanny like Janet, didn't need to sense anything outside the reach of his own physical capacities through curtains of oblivion. He was a thoroughly unalarming little boy, full of expression, rich with responses. He just couldn't speak.

And it was hurting him.

This was when my mother-in-law asked, "Do you think it might be a reaction to all the stress of the last couple of years?"

I reviewed: the sequence of personal and institutional events that had placed me, at thirty-two, as chair of the English department at the height of faculty warfare. My preoccupations with departmental concerns in my conversations with my husband. Mark's increasing desperation at being the stay-home parent, with an increasingly distant spouse, my deepening anger at feeling no alternatives. My urgent wish to leave Alpine, Utah, my hometown, behind with my religion. His equally passionate wish to raise our children here, geographically a city of dreams, and to hold as well as he could to his heritage of faith. Ugly political developments in Alpine that directly and publicly affected my father and his family. Mark's wish to build a house, the one he had been planning for years, the one that meant we were settled, irrevocably, on a lot we owned in Alpine. My wish to write something besides inter-office memos. Shocking, screaming arguments, shaking the foundations of the stable world we had so carefully built around our young children.

And, in the heart of it all, a surprise pregnancy. Through an interminable segment of it, Mark stayed with the kids while I went to work, stayed at his parents' thirty miles away when I came home. We couldn't speak. Couldn't let our eyes meet.

Porter, demonstrably sensitive to body language, certainly picked up plenty of pain. Can pain paralyze one form of communication, even as it unleashes another?

We went back into marriage therapy. For a while we met separately, with different therapists, then met together, the four of us. Gary and Sally coached us carefully, sentence by sentence, as we learned to speak again. We played games. Speak only when you hold the "talking stick." Hand it to him after sixty seconds.

Try to respond directly to what she's saying, before you go on to the next issue.

Stop now, and acknowledge his anger.

It's only a game. It's a symbol, too, just like a word. Let it be what it is.

Five weeks before the baby was due, I went to South Carolina to attend a conference for the college. We used the occasion as a chance for Mark to settle back in. Mark, Amelia, Christian, and Porter met me at the Delta wing, drove me home. The school year ended a week after that, and I finalized plans for a one-year personal leave of absence. We made the imminent arrival of our fourth child a final reason to retire our well-used camping tent and buy a little fold-out trailer, complete with stove and refrigerator, beds for everyone and a collapsible eating table. We spent the week before the baby was born on the San Rafael Swell, comfortable as eight months and three weeks pregnant could be for any of us. We sat peaceably on the banks of the San Juan River, perpendicular orange cliffs above us. We pondered the snaky ghostly Barrier Canyon petroglyphs. Half hoping it would put me in labor, I walked with Mark and the kids to the precipice of Black Box Canyon. We sat on a ledge, ten feet square, keeping a grip on small shirts and hiking shorts and the small bodies inside of them as we ate crackers and cheese, the San Juan coursing 600 vertical feet below. Back at camp, Porter reveled in the sunlight, shamelessly shed his clothes to splash in the shallows, sang out loud to the moon, devoured his morning pancakes.

We named the baby "Maya," for lots of reasons, not the least of which was that it is easy to say. Porter loved her instantly, still after twenty months insists that really she's his own baby. His first perfect word was her name.

Speech therapy perplexes me. I wondered when we first took him how it was that a speech therapist might proceed. I guess I was hoping for something mysterious yet efficacious. It's actually pretty unmysterious. It's drill and practice, one sound at a time, one sound position at a time. "P," for instance, is easiest to make as a sound when it's at the end of a word. So we start with "p" sounds at the ends of words. We practice for two weeks.

Therapist: "Cap."
Porter: "'ak."
Therapist: "Watch my lips, Porter. Cap."
Porter: "'ak—puh."
Therapist: "Okay. Nap."
Porter: "'ak—puh." He held my hand as we walked back out to the

Wrangler to drive home.

"What's that, Porter?" I asked.

"'Eek—puh."

We go on, if we can stay systematic, to other final consonant sounds, one at a time, two-week intervals. Then we have to re-learn "p" as a middle-of-the-word sound. Speech therapy breaks up the sounds and positions into the tiniest possible components, teaches them one at a time, again and again, over weeks and sometimes years. Practice and drill. Watch my tongue. Speech therapy teaches a child like Porter the smallest mechanisms of what Amelia and Christian seemed to produce spontaneously, the same way they grew fingers and toes. Look at my teeth, Porter. On my lips. "Flat tire" sound. We break up the monotony with games, an alligator with pushable teeth, say, or bright-colored tokens to move along the spaces on a board.

Something mysterious and efficacious did begin to occur, actually, although I do not understand how it sprang from speech therapy, or from a different family season, or from genetic designs and traces of neural paths. Porter started to make intelligible words. Not as fast as they might come for a natural speaker, but a heck of a lot quicker than the therapy calendar.

He has a pattern. I've watched it seven or eight times now. His language goes backward for a day or so. He loses almost all intelligibility. He cries with frustration, sweats at his temples just trying to make simple words. He's exhausted, physically and emotionally, by five or six in the evening. He sleeps hard, cries out, goes back under. Wakes up with a breakthrough, a new set of sounds, a clear mind. The speech therapist said to watch him closely at times like that, to speak to him in clear, simple sentences, giving him plenty of time to respond. Otherwise he could develop a stammer, too much too fast.

So far he's holding steady.

Porter is almost five years old. At home he's constantly talking, long sentences with abstractions of time, imagination, and possibility. I sometimes have to remind myself not to tell him to hush a minute. He's cunning and calculating enough to negotiate his way through any sibling negotiation, even with the disadvantage of youth. His shrewd reading of nonverbal signals gives him the advantage of seeming to know what's going on in an unfamiliar situation. He's quick and funny with a joke. "YUCK! OO AWTED?" He giggles in the bathtub with Christian, after squeezing the rubber duck under the water.

He asks questions, urgently, as if he were catching up for a long season of silent curiosity. "Mom, how does waddo make you wet?" "How do 'ey make aopwanes?" "When I 'et big, will my name s'ill be 'oto 'out?"

He points out the "oowuck oowacks" on the snowy street.

He tells me, "I made a new oo-wend at ees—ool ooday."

I ask him, "Was it a boy or girl?"

"Oo—wo."

"What's her name?"

"Ay—wo"

"Taylor? Did you have a nice time playing with Taylor?"

We stop for doughnuts every morning that we drive to work and pre-school. It's a standing deal with Porter. "Unwess we aw wate," he concedes, generously, for his mama's sake.

But he shuts down in public. His pre-school and Sunday school teachers tell us he's extremely shy. In a strange environment, he is. He has a way of turning his eyes to a fascinating brick on the wall, of studying his dimpled nail-bitten fingers, and tuning out any foreign inquiries. He just doesn't respond, not at all, not a flicker in his flashy green eyes.

And talking, even when he's on a roll, taxes him. Words, phrases, comebacks, questions, authority fly like magic from the lips of his older siblings. Maya, at twenty months, says fifteen reasonably intelligible words. It's not hard to see the language gathering in her, like a swirling reservoir, and it's clear to all of us, maybe especially Porter, that the floodgates are about to open.

For the last two or three weeks Porter has been carrying a heavy old 35mm camera around his neck, one that I used years ago and never had fixed once it broke. It doesn't look broken, though, and the shutter snaps with a satisfying sequence of clicks. It winds clean and snaps again. Porter asked if he could have it for his very own. He loves mechanical objects. He snaps pictures all over the house. Pictures of Maya eating cereal. Pictures of me in the kitchen, or at the computer. Our new house, a beautiful one, built by an artist for his own four children, has a separate studio twenty feet across the driveway. Porter puts on his boots and coat, trudges the snowy distance, opens the door with a frantically suppressed giggle, sneaks the camera into the opening and takes his shot. He catches Christian and Amelia from the front porch as they come home from the bus stop. They grin and wave. There's no film, but the sound of the shutter freezes an image for me, every time. Maybe for Porter, too. Someday I will buy him a real camera, a really fine camera.

Oliver Sacks describes, in much of his writing, the ability of the human mind to find alternative paths for intelligence, create remarkable compensations for broken functions. I keep thinking of the old irrigation system in Alpine, a complex and beautiful series of dams and headgates, almost endlessly interchangeable in their routes and channels. Some of my best memories of childhood come from the nights my dad let me get up with him for a late-night water turn. We'd trace the ditches to each dry headgate, pulling the gate and placing it in another slot, cleaning debris and fortifying with dirt and sand. Dad would say, "Listen for the water now. It's probably at Bennett's gate," and suddenly we would hear it, pull the dam, re-route the cold, black, perfect water toward our orchard, follow it down until it roared at our turn-gate, dropped through the rusted culvert under the street, rose to the level of our trees, and spilled back out into the moonlight.

I can't love my dad in quite the same way I did then. But Porter can. Porter knows how. And we couldn't imagine how Janet would survive without her mother. Elaine has been dead of cancer for more than half a year. A month before Elaine died, my two sisters and I stayed with Janet while her family attended a wedding. We danced to "Itsy-Bitsy Teeny-Weeny Yellow Polka-Dot Bikini." Boy, did we. Two and a half hours. Janet lunged and gyrated, leaped and boogied. Threw her arms, swung her hips, flipped her head. So did I, like I never did in my life. Janet seems to be getting on with her father and grown-up siblings pretty well.

Mark and I can have long conversations, even painful ones, that actually seem to nourish something between us, and we can do it without the talking stick.

And Porter speaks. He's making his own maps, covering territory we can't follow him through, breaking his own trails, following the tributaries. I'm learning another kind of faith, and watching for signals.

Fighting with My Mother

Susan Elizabeth Howe

My mother, riding
next to me as I drive,
watches at stop signs.
She's looking right
for dangers
that might have an impact
on our relative positions
in the car.
Trying to avoid
accidents, she says,
"Clear right."
Looking left, I ask
myself shall I trust
our lives to her
judgment? or
turn to see
for myself?
"Still clear. Clear right."
However long
I hold my eyes
left, or straight,
I finally turn my stiff
neck to see
what she says isn't
coming. But
sometimes it is.

Pennyroyal, Cohosh, Rue

Julie Nichols

ABOUT THE TIME I FIRST REALIZED I was a feminist, I went
to a women's retreat at a little mountain spa an hour's drive from the
ultra-Mormon town where I was living at the time. The retreat, one of
those such as are advertised in *New Age Journal* and the spirituality is-
sues of *Ms.*, attracted about a hundred women who were willing to
dance their self-portraits, choose new names in a rebirthing ceremony,
and sit in mooncircles and meditate. Tom, my husband, wary of this
feminist spirituality, said it was nothing but big business, too much les-
bianism, too much separateness. There was evidence in LDS church
history for discussion of a Mother in Heaven, he said, who probably
headed the Relief Society or some similar celestial female organization,
but the private circles, the rituals and healings by laying-on of female
hands—those were definitely anti-church, anti-family, and anti-
Christ. But I loved them, because they were so much inward work in
contrast to the hectic externalities of my life as a working Mormon
mother.

During one of the mooncircles at the retreat, the leaders, whose
names were Roberta and Mary Lou, instructed us to visualize two
women we trusted coming to us, dressing us in robes, and leading us to
a temple where we were to meet the Goddess ourselves. This was
deeply moving for me chiefly because of the two women who came to
me. One was my mother, who died when I was very small but who
comes to me often in dreams, seeming to love me always even when I
rebel against certain church policies, even the ones I have thought she
would hold most sacred.

The other woman who came to me in this exercise of the imagination was my late Grandma Jean, the most orthodox of her orthodox
generation, the reputable and honored wife of the patriarch of the

Maynard clan. Her coming, full of unmistakable warmth and approval, to dress me in pagan robes and lead me to a decidedly non-Mormon temple, indicated to me more surely than my mother's appearance that this meditation was not a product of my imagination. In my wildest dreams I would not have conjured this up. I figure I have a right to claim my mother's unconditional love, but Grandma Jean's? She was a straight one. She'd not have stood for some of the things I've done.

Yet during the meditation she stayed with me, closer and brighter than my mother, and when it was time to return to normal consciousness, it was her embrace that sent me back. I could only sit with my head bowed against my knees, there on the floor of the mountain spa lodge, when Roberta and Mary Lou asked us to share. I couldn't speak.

Grandma Jean had been a beautiful, tall woman, slim-waisted, full-breasted, white-haired in her last years like a queen. My other grandmother had bowed to osteoporosis (I took megadoses of calcium to prevent the same fate in my own bones) and had died brittle and bent, but Jean stood straight and met your eye fully, even when she was eighty-eight and hadn't long to live. She was a gifted storyteller, much in demand at socials, holding adults and children alike in thrall repeating "The Cask of Amontillado" from memory, or "A Child's Christmas in Wales," or the story of Joseph and the coat of many colors, somehow making connections between that Joseph and our Joseph in the grove at Palmyra.

We who were her grandchildren were also treated to other stories, personal rather than community ones, about the misadventures of our parents and uncles and aunts. To me, they were entertainment of the highest order, though they made me feel that I could never live up to Grandma Jean's standards, either of respectability or of fun. My generation was hopeless. All the good times and all the need for serious, responsible behavior because of the burden of life had already been used up by her children and their friends, or by her own friends, whose stories she told more rarely.

It was one of these, however, that made the deepest impression on me, and helped me to understand something of why she came in my imagination to that retreat, and why I couldn't speak after.

Grandma Jean was the child of a polygamist. Her youth was full of children and "aunts," "but," she told me, "we were rich. We weren't like some of these fundamentalists you see around today, dozens of children and no income, just rags and hungry eyes. Land, no! Eighteen of us lived in the same house, but it had ten bedrooms and two parlors, up there in Morgan, and our mothers got along wonderfully well. We were luckier than most."

Luckier especially than the Caldwells. Grandma's best friend in those days was Beleatha Caldwell, third child of the first wife of Heber. They were both ten years old when Brother Caldwell married two young sisters on the same day, just a month after Beleatha's mother died leaving seven children. Both of these new wives were fertile as rabbits, Grandma Jean said, conjuring up in my mind images of fluffy children hopping around a grassy side yard chewing lettuce and carrots. In five years there were seven more Caldwells. Beleatha and Jean used to sit on the fence bordering Brother Caldwell's pasture and giggle about the diapers draped everywhere to dry. When the older of the two "new" wives caught smallpox in the epidemic of 1908 and died, the other, Prudence, with Caldwell Number Fifteen "in the oven," as Grandma put it, took on primary responsibility for them all, and then for the farm as well when Brother Caldwell was called on a mission to England. Jean saw Beleatha less and less as she was needed more and more to watch the little ones and help with meals and housework, though she still got away from time to time and giggled as much as ever when she did.

Until the time Jean went over just in time to see Beleatha trying to hold Prudence back while Prudence slashed at some chickens in the yard, chopping right and left with the old axe, feathers and blood everywhere and horrible squawking, not just from the chickens but from Prudence too. This was no ordinary butchering, Grandma said; there was something disorderly about it, frightening and wasteful, and she never could quite bring herself to mention it to Beleatha, but ran home quickly before she was seen.

This was just before Michael Adam, the baby, was born. After that, Grandma said, Beleatha never came out to giggle by the fence and the Caldwell children began to look increasingly ragged and strange.

One day Peggy May, the nine-year-old, came to school in one of Prudence's temple garments rolled up and pinned together. The teacher hustled her over to Sister Carpenter's in a twinkling and they put something else on her, but nobody had missed the long-sleeved underwear dragging in Peggy's wake. Another day Sam, who was two, was seen toddling across the canal bridge, trailing his diapers and wailing for all he was worth. Sister Rosas brought him home to her house and kept him for a week.

The oldest Caldwell boy, Matt, had a hard time keeping up with the farm. Naturally most of the men tried to come lend a hand, and the next brother, William, did the best he could to help, but during the summer harvest Prudence got on the buckboard and flogged one of the horses to death. Then she left it lying in the middle of the field and took herself into the house to bed. It was difficult for anybody to know what to do after that. Nobody wanted his own horses overworked, and the family seemed less and less inclined to accept help anyway.

"'Pathetic' was a soft word for it," Grandma Jean said. "The bishop refused to send for Brother Caldwell off his mission. Of course, it would have taken months to get the word to him and get him home anyway, but he should have been told what was happening to his wife and household. Beleatha looked grimmer and grimmer and the other fourteen kids did too. Grim and ragged. It was obvious to everyone that Prudence was losing her mind."

The day Prudence shot the babies it was summer's end. Most ladies were home canning tomatoes and pickles, checking melons for ripeness, sending the children off to play at the canal under the watchful eye of Missy Praetor, who'd been to the coast and knew how to swim well enough to save lives if need be. William Caldwell had brought in a load of hay the day before and figured he deserved a break, so he was down at the canal making eyes at Missy. Beleatha had come away too. She and Jean were picking the blackberries that bore like crazy along the pasture fences.

"Things seemed gratefully calm for the moment," Grandma said. "All afternoon I'd seen the Caldwell kids coming in and out of the house, some with what I thought were bundles of wash, one or two with boxes. Then I heard a high unusual sound. Like a baby moaning. Beleatha and I could see Prudence come to the door with the baby hanging over one arm and one of her sister's children hanging over the other. Remember, Prudence couldn't have been more than twenty-four, and that baby—the youngest of fifteen, ten of whom were under nine—was about three months old. He'd been colicky, too, poor thing. Even the midwife's peppermint tinctures didn't help his screaming.

"Prudence came to the door like that and Beleatha said, 'Oh-oh, she's going to want me now,' and started picking up her buckets and getting ready to go in. But it was the oddest thing. Prudence just stood there in the door. Not calling. Not anything. She looked left and right, away from us, and then she turned around and kind of staggered back inside and shut the door. Beleatha and I remarked how quiet it suddenly seemed. No children. No animals. I remember Beleatha whispered, 'Dear Lord!' and at the exact same moment we heard two sharp shots from inside the house.

"Beleatha didn't even pick up her things. She was out of those berry bushes in two leaps—I tore after her through the weedy garden and across the doorstep in less time than it takes to tell—the door was locked—we pounded on the west window till it fell open and I pushed Beleatha up through it. I can still see her patched underwear like it was yesterday. And when I scrambled up after her and got inside, I wished I hadn't, because there in a puddle of blood lay the baby Michael Adam, and the other baby—I think its name was Jennifer—sat staring in a corner with its mouth open and no sound.

"They were dead as doornails. And Prudence held the gun to her chest like a cross.

"Beleatha screamed. I thought she'd never quit. But then William came, and several of the men, and they took Prudence and those two pathetic bodies, and after that women started to come in to the house, one every day, leaving their own families as if they didn't have enough to do, and the children got fed and taken care of and eventually Beleatha more or less became the mother, although she never had to do it all alone. The Relief Society saw to that. Brother Caldwell came home but it wasn't till months later, and I don't think anyone in Morgan forgave him for not coming home the minute he heard."

"Why did Prudence do it, Grandma Jean?" I asked.

If Grandma had been a lesser woman she might have shrugged, might have put me off to ponder it for myself. But she was regal—a Maynard—and she gave it to me straight. "Well, child, some said it was the heat. Land, it *was* a hot summer. And some blamed the bishop, too, for sending off Heber Caldwell in the first place.

"But I know another thing or two.

"Beleatha told me Prudence aspired to be a midwife—a noble profession then and now, more trusted by smart women than men doctors any time. She told Beleatha that if she could know what midwives knew, she could handle any situation that came up. And the way Beleatha said 'situation,' I knew Prudence meant things I was supposedly too young to have wind of. What I think was, Prudence just got trapped. She saw herself backed into a corner too tight and too deep ever to come whole out of, all of her life drifting away in diapers and dust. That's what those bundles were that the little Caldwells were taking out of the house before the shooting—Prudence had sent them down to the canal with bundles of clean diapers. She'd told them to throw them in. That was how William knew something was wrong and came back when he did."

"She did it because she was crazy," said my mother's sister, Marta, who was ten years older than I and was listening in.

"Well, child, it's a toss-up who was crazier, Prudence or the bishop, for sending off Heber, or old Heber himself, to leave, even on the Lord's work, and set a young pregnant woman to brood over a farm and fifteen little ones. Seems like a strange definition of the Lord's work, to leave such a burden on anyone knowingly. I hold them all to blame. I get mighty sick of seeing men let women try to handle any yoke the men lay on their shoulders. I thought—still think—it was Caldwell should have been shot, and Prudence brought back to normal life with the gentlest of care."

"What happened to Beleatha?"

"She became a midwife," my grandmother said. But by then her attention was wavering. Grandma Jean involved herself totally when she was in the midst of a story, but once it was over, it was over. She was a Relief Society president, after all, and her duties were many. It was only later and quite by accident that I ever heard any more about Beleatha Caldwell.

On a Saturday a few months after the retreat, my husband, my Aunt Marta, and I were standing around her sink doing something to a huge bag of potatoes, getting them ready to bake for a Maynard family gathering. Tom and I attended these parties loyally. Since coming out of the closet about women holding the priesthood, abortion rights, and certain other very anti-patriarchal convictions, I had had to come to terms with the fact that I still wanted to hold fast to certain traditions. Partly for the children, of course—my Christopher and Katie needed some family ties, and the Maynards gave them water balloons along with everyone else and we all spit watermelon seeds in the yearly contest and it was all very family and I quit apologizing to myself or anyone else for doing something so Mormon as attending a family reunion.

As we washed and slit the potatoes this time, then, the topic of conversation rolled around to Liza, Aunt Marta's teenaged daughter who had just miscarried a fetus conceived out of wedlock.

"A lucky break," I said.

"Riva," my husband said, disapproving. "Marta's broken-hearted. Aren't you?" Marta, in from California, scrubbed more vigorously.

I felt heartless though. "Why?" I said. "It wasn't your baby." As if she weren't there. But then I thought Marta often wasn't, even when she was.

However, "It would have been if it had been born," she said. Sadly.

"And did you want that? I wouldn't." Such bravery. If Grandma Jean had been there, I'd have never said it.

"You'd reject your own grandchild?" Tom said, trying my patience, pushing the envelope, scrubbing the spuds.

"Well, I wouldn't want to raise it," I said. "I've had enough raising my own children." This is out in the open between us; why not make it so for all the Maynards to know? "I don't need to raise another generation."

Then Marta surprised me. "Would *you* raise it?" she asked Tom.

"I wouldn't have to," he said. Then he realized what he'd said and grabbed another potato and stabbed it thirty or forty times with the point end of his knife, to divert our attention, I suppose. Marta and I met each other's eyes. There were tears in hers.

"I'm sorry," I said. I meant it.

"Oh, heavens, don't flatter yourself," she said, suddenly back to normal, brisk and conventional. "Do you think that bothers me all that much? I'm sorry to be so drippy. It's just that suddenly you reminded me of my mother. Did you know that? You always did." She handed me a bowl of potatoes and gestured toward the oven. Time for them to go in. "I found some papers last month—imagine, after five years! You might be interested in them. I'll give them to you after everyone leaves.

"Lon'd take them if he saw them," she said. "He figures everything of Mother's should go to him, him being the oldest and all. But I don't want him to know. I consider you to be the one to have them. See if you can decipher why. Tell me if it's what you think."

The children fell asleep in the back of the station wagon on the way home that night, so I pulled out the oversized envelope Marta had given me just before we left, as Tom drove south on I-15 through the soft gray summer twilight. In the packet were several small plastic bags with what looked like a layer of dirt in them, and several ruled pages, torn as if from a ledger, covered with Grandma's even, upright handwriting.

There was little of interest to Lon or anyone else in these pages, I thought at first. They were dated during several weeks in a spring of the Depression, years before I was born and just after Marta turned two. Marta was the youngest of Grandma's nine children, the one who consistently spit watermelon seeds the farthest to win the prize of cherry bonbons, which I coveted. Everyone in the family knew how Grandma had struggled to go to nursing school during the Depression and had earned her LPN certificate; it was because of this training, I thought, that she had taught me to wash my hands so thoroughly, to maintain my "female sanitation," as she put it, and to keep careful track of my cycles. I sometimes thought she was a little fanatical, but I assumed that was typical of one trained during that period. Everyone also knew that Grandpa had been promoted to a lucrative (for those days) traveling job shortly after she got her license, so that Grandma Jean had elected to stay home and be a live-in parent instead of a working one. She was proud of this choice, proud of the "jewels" that were her children, proud of the ways she'd put her skills and talents to work at home and in the church. I'd been raised not only listening to Grandma's stories, but also eating her homemade bread, sleeping under her quilts, and playing with her plaster-headed dolls, hand-molded and hand-painted. In the family she was held up as womanhood perfected—domestic, creative, organized, content. I knew from an early age I would never live up to her image.

I read aloud to my husband from the ledger pages for several miles. They were much like a modern Relief Society president's Day-Timer might be; I was lulled half to sleep by the rhythm of people to visit, dinners to arrange, meetings to attend, funerals to oversee.

Then, on a Thursday, this notation:

> *Today is Day 30 of my cycle. I cannot be THAT WAY again—so much to do, so little money, Maynard so seldom at home. Beleatha Caldwell*

—and an Ogden address.

I read on silently to myself.

> *Friday. Day 31. Beleatha says: 2X pennyroyal, X cohosh, X rue. 3x/day. The tea tastes vile but I will not stop taking it.*
>
> *Day 33. No one must know. I take the tea quickly when no one will see. What would the bishop say? Maynard must have no inkling.*
>
> *Day 39. I am hateful today. Screamed as though possessed at little Marta. I believe this anger is female in origin. I hope to know soon.*
>
> *Day 40. Blood. Thank God. I will hide all the evidence, but I would do it again. Oh how I thank my God!*

Your god is my Goddess, I thought. I folded the papers back into their creases and, in a gesture millennia of women old, I tucked them deep into a hidden place in my purse.

"Anything interesting?" said my husband.

"A recipe," I said. "That's about all."

A few days after that I called the health food store and asked them about pennyroyal. Estrogen, they said. Good for hot flashes. Cohosh? Yes, also a female tonic. Good stuff. Rue? We don't carry that. So I called another friend, a healer who works with crystals and gemstones and also knows herbs.

"They're excellent female strengtheners," she said, "unless you're pregnant. Any of them will cause miscarriage. Why?"

"I found them growing in my life," I told her. Then I called Marta.

"It's what you thought," I said.

"Will you take care of those papers? Will you burn them?"

"I'll take care of them," I said. "I'll burn them." And I did. But the story needs to be written. Lon need never know, the bishop need never hear. Grandpa will have no inkling. But our daughters should be told. The courage of our mothers—the grace of the Goddess to those who say no for their own good and the glory of She Who Is One-in-Herself—these things must not be forgotten.

The Shadow Side of Mothering

Julie Nichols

ABOUT THE TIME I BECAME A mother for the third time, I began to feel a certain kind of panic—and a certain kind of disbelief that there are mothers who can keep having children and *not* feel as trapped as I. "Pennyroyal, Cohosh, Rue" was written after my fourth child was born, and after I met a couple of women who had used the very recipe in the story to terminate pregnancies in a private and noninvasive way. I understood why they did it, and I wanted to write something about Mormon women—who are my women, after all—who were faithful and obedient and yet empowered enough to take control of their reproductive life. I wanted to show how Grandma Maynard could approve of feminism, and to suggest a possible justification for such approval in her witnessing of Prudence's story. I wanted hearts to ache for Prudence, who had no support but whose situation was really no different from mine, only more exaggerated. In fiction the rule is: exaggerate the conflict in order to justify the resolution.

But in real life there's no need to exaggerate the conflict. Children are a blessing—we're told this from the time we're children ourselves. I'm telling the truth when I say that for me there is nothing in the universe like holding a newborn baby—nothing. Utter magic. *However*, at the same time I heard that children would be my crown and my glory, I also heard "You can do whatever you want to," "God gave you gifts so you could serve the Kingdom of God," and "Your talents are your greatest assets." I excelled academically my whole life, won awards and recognition, and based much of my feeling of self-worth on my ability to think and write and speak. I loved to read, and I wanted to share this love, both as a student and as a teacher. It never seemed at all logical that I should give up this love for children, and I never intended to.

So I played superwoman till that third child came. I attended graduate school, wrote scholarly and creative pieces, and taught at the university while I was a young wife bearing those babies. About five years into my marriage, I nearly had a nervous breakdown—about the time I had two preschool sons and a colicky sleepless new daughter and a husband whose job didn't provide adequately for us, so that I also taught at the university to keep food on the table. I have a clear memory of standing in my front yard watching the boys tumble and play with half the other neighborhood children while the baby screamed herself purple, and being paralyzed by exhaustion and tears. My elderly neighbor saw me weeping helplessly and in a gesture that seems now to me to be the epitome of kindness, she picked up my baby and rocked her and suggested I go inside and rest. Reality would not let me play at being superwoman any longer.

In the LDS church we don't like to focus much on what Jung called "the Shadow." In 1992 and 1993 I received counseling and training in a psychological technique called "Voice Dialogue," developed and described in detail by Drs. Hal and Sidra Stone in their books *Embracing Our Selves, Embracing Each Other* and *Embracing Your Inner Critic*. Briefly, the theory is that each of us identifies with certain primary "voices" which we tend to think we *are*. For me, and for many Mormon women, I suspect, that primary voice is "traditional mother/wife." For me, duty and hard work were the only pathways to what I felt responsible Mormon womanhood compelled me to be: a wife who filled in where her husband lacked, and a mother who made sure her children were provided for physically, mentally, emotionally, and socially *regardless of what happened to my own heart, my own soul, in the meantime*. "My own heart, my own soul" would be satisfied by my ability to achieve this goal, or so I understood the official story to say.

But according to the doctors Stone, the first law of physics—that for every action there is an equal and opposite reaction—prevails in our personalities as well. In each of us there is a "disowned voice" for every "primary voice"—a voice that yearns for expression, and that makes us ill if it is not embraced by an aware consciousness. It's precisely the principle Jesus was following when he said to those who would destroy the adulteress, "Let the person who is without sin cast the first stone": we have in us the potential for *every* kind of behavior, and if we deny this we deny ourselves the potential for Christlike compassion.

Let me explain. During those first five years of my marriage I denied any "voice" in me but the traditional mother/wife voice—which for me meant that I denied not only any angry or desperate or frightened part of me (since a good wife and mother is in control all the time, especially if she's been a bright and capable person all her life), but also that I denied any part of me that could have spontaneous, irresponsible fun. I denied myself my own kind of play, though I took my children to the park often enough and pushed them on swings and sat with them on the floor at home and built Lego creations and read them the entire *Wizard of Oz* series and taught them songs and sewed them Halloween costumes, and the list goes on and on. I played—but I didn't play for the part of me that remembered my own childhood, my own love for solitude, for good novels, for crazy friends who made me laugh with their puns and their skits and their love of things political and cultural. These things got pushed away—"disowned"—by that mother/wife voice.

But as hard as a primary voice pushes away a disowned voice, to that same degree the disowned voice will push back somehow. Sometimes it comes out in illness—mental, emotional, or physical. Sometimes it comes out in unexpected outbursts—you know, the "where did *that* come from?" kind, when a normally placid wife screams at her husband that he never understood her and she just has to get away and she's leaving, now, and he can just see how it feels to be home alone with these three little kids all day long! That kind. That's a disowned self pushing back.

According to the Stones, health is restored when the disowned voice is embraced again. This does *not* mean that the furious mother leaves the family forever and becomes a wild party animal hopping bars and picking up men. Far from it. It means that she listens to the voice that says, "I'm tired ... I'm lonely for my own kind of friend, my own kind of stimulation ... I miss my single life, my life as a student ..." That's all. She *listens* to it. She *hears* it. She pays attention to it as she pays attention to her own children, and gives it what it needs, in appropriate doses.

If she doesn't, it will strike back.

And yet most of us don't know how to listen to our disowned voices—our Shadows. We think we must keep them suppressed—we think they're evil, that they'll distract us from our duty, that they'll cause us to be reprimanded, punished, perhaps that if we listen to them we'll lose everything we've worked so hard to have. So we don't dare hear them, much less give them what they ask for—a little peace, a little time to relax, a little of what gives them juice and joy and nurturing. We don't realize that we can listen to them *and* to our primary voices too—that we're supporting our full, round souls when we listen to *both*. "There must needs be an opposition in all things"—Nephi's not saying this just so we can be stoic through hard times. He's saying that for every primary voice, there's a disowned voice that needs attention, and that proper listening will help to heal us. Embracing *all* of our selves is the only way to be whole.

Now one of the problems is that the culture doesn't support these disowned voices very much. My husband didn't know what I needed any more than I did. We both thought we were doing exactly what we were supposed to be doing by having three babies in four years and another one not long after that. Neither one of us was particularly happy; neither one of us felt that our life was "fun"; but we felt that we were doing what we were supposed to be doing, so we disowned the parts of ourselves that longed for a little free time, a little adult stimulation, a little of what gave us joy before we were ever married.

Yet these Shadows, these disowned voices, were always waiting. And when I finally reached a point of vulnerability that day in my front yard, I knew I had to at least admit that I was overburdened. That my cup was neither full nor overflowing, but constantly draining. That I had no idea how to help myself, because I had three small children who constantly needed me to help them. My Shadow flew up in my face, and I knew why a Prudence might shoot her babies, I knew why Grandma Maynard terminated her tenth pregnancy. I knew why people flee from this thing called motherhood.

Two more statements are necessary here. First: my third and fourth children were born at home, in a remarkably supportive environment with the help of gifted intuitive midwives. I wouldn't trade these experiences for anything. Holding my babies, gazing at their beauty, and nursing them many months each, are precious memories, precious feelings I would never trade. Three of them are now teenagers and the fourth is in that wonderful can-do-for-himself-but-isn't-yet-obnoxious preteen stage, and I'm proud to be their mother and amazed at the range of their talents and interests. I would never trade motherhood for motherlessness. I'm profoundly grateful for the experience.

Second, however, and this is the heart of my "disclaimer" for "Pennyroyal, Cohosh, Rue": I don't know how to make things easier for young mothers. It's too easy, it's too pat to say "Young mothers need time off and should allow it for themselves." In the first place, none of the young mothers I know in Mormondom have it in them to just leave their children. They worry about childcare, but more than that they believe, as I did, that what they do for their own souls is frivolous, not as important, not as worthwhile, as what they do for their children. I know this guilt. I know the superwoman syndrome. I bought into it wholeheartedly. One of my hopes for our culture is that we can embrace economic and human reality and not require more of any of us than we can honestly bear.

And though I would never tell anyone not to have a child, and I would *not* recommend abortion to anyone—though these are true statements, *still I believe I know why a woman would choose not to have a child, and I honor that voice in each of us.* This is why I wrote "Pennyroyal, Cohosh, Rue": because there is a dark side to each of us that we must embrace. For if we do not, it will come back to haunt us—in small bursts of discourtesy, in barely controlled bouts of impatience, in growing uncontrollable anger, in downright neglect and abuse—of our children and ourselves. It was important to write about this part of me—of all women, I think—who appeared in my life so strongly and so fiercely shortly after my last child was born; important to write about her in order to know how to deal with her in appropriate and compassionate ways.

I hoped, as I wrote, that I could show not that abortion is good or that child-killing is good, but only how either is possible. I hoped only to honor in myself a voice I would never express in physical action. For me, as it always is, writing parts of myself into fiction was an act of compassionate exorcism. My reward has been not a worry-free, guilt-free motherhood—not at all! It has been a richer, more honest creative life. The Maynards are the focus of the novel I am currently writing, and it has taken me into life more widely than my traditional mother voice would ever let me go. I am grateful to them forever.

Getting Away
How It Happens Again and Again

Dixie Lee Partridge

Digging in bright sand, my son at five
is struck by what his brother tells him:
light of the stars already old,
the sun's rising several moments
before he feels the lick of warmth
across his face.

They sit in the hole they have dug,
sifting warm sand onto their bellies.
Beside me in the shade of ancient black rock
their sister sleeps, lips slightly parted
over the metal of braces, her face
turned toward me in open amnesia.

A breeze whips up a shower of sand
but she sleeps on. My sons' voices continue
non-stop, the wind lifting syllables
like small, white petals
I catch only glimpses of.

We come here because the shore
is the one place we can do nothing
without boredom or guilt:
whether it's the constancy of the tides
washing through us again and again,
we let go of everything
to lounge in what we want to believe.

Traces of sand have settled
in my daughter's ear, over the curve
of her eyelid. The sun nears the horizon
of the other side of the world,
cities and continents driven with energies

suddenly staggering. For a moment
the plot of the earth's story
shifts toward me ...
that white dune, fear.

All Day at 30 Degrees

Dixie Lee Partridge

> "The melting and freezing points of a sub-
> stance are the same."
> —my daughter's science class notes

Still white out.
It can go either way—
like that rim before tears,
like her silence:

> my seventeen-year daughter runs
> in all weather, skipping meals
> to grow lean.

> We've repeated the ritual:
> *Dinner's almost on ...*
> *Later, Mom, ...*
> the closing of the front door.

There's a point of exertion
when one more movement will bring a dew
to the brow.
The moving beauty of water
curved above the cup's lip
spills down all sides
with one more drop.

139

Last night I looked up the word
anorexia, found it comes from the Greek
meaning *without reaching out*.

Now with a feline caution
I follow her outside, but don't know
what to call after her,
her two-mile route into blue light.

Not yet a syllable from the eaves
to start the windows singing.
Under the far albino sun,
blue stones of creekbeds
are open mouths in the snow.

Her tall, thin form,
her pale skin and hair,
dissolve into a milky distance.

Falling Asleep, After the Wedding

Dixie Lee Partridge

You think of friends talking in the yard
in summer dresses and suits, and it's like
looking over your shoulder into a brief past you're leaving
for something else. Your son and his bride,

unreal and beautiful, pose still
for photographs. You turn
and see your mother clearing off tables
of the wedding reception, and you don't remember

to think she's a thousand miles away on the farm
and couldn't come. There's your father, too,
in his bib overalls ...
He's eating wedding cake and is not

supposed to have sugar, and will be sick.
Your mother looks young and hands you plates
that you carry to the farmhouse sink where the water pressure
is only a drip because someone is taking a bath

and it's your father. The knob to the bathroom door
is still broken, and before you complete the thought
about growing up believing that when something breaks
you must live with it, get by, your grown children

come into the kitchen, muddied in their formal clothes,
and you don't know where to send them
to clean up, and why would they listen to you anyway
doing dishes still after breakfast, oatmeal caked in the pan.

Your mother puts newspapers over the floor
for them to stand on, and simply waits with her most patient face
for you to do something, and you only know to keep on
stiffly washing dishes. She finally says why can't you just

use your dishwasher, and you feel foolish because
you can't quite remember what's between this sink
and your house in birch trees and dogwood,
reception flowers, the dishwasher.

And now your limbs seem on the verge
of melting—something lets go
to relinquish the body that tries to do what needs to be done
to the one that can't do much at all, as if

this version of being is what you need to love,
and even though everything else does matter,
you will not be able to sort things out
in the lifespan of dreams.

Charm for a Sick Child

Linda Sillitoe

we will dream now of a cave
with a figure at the entrance.
see the magic seeds she holds

to twinkle new stars into your
angry blood. two fingers cross
your wrist, then above your head

my hand traces the entrance;
dream beginning and end
as you swelter in bed.

remember the godmother
little one.
pockets of glass slippers
and surprise home runs
your wishes hover here
like candle smoke

the wave not the wand is potent.
and godmother mothergod mother
will bring you seawater, sun

and thunder, a fresh start.
what in my bones knit you
within me still weaves magic.

sleep now. here is the sign
more ancient than memory.
here is the turn in the tide.

Red Roses for a Blue Lady

Carol B. Quist

ON A COLD, CLEAR AFTERNOON in February 1968, I drove
with baby Kenneth from West Caldwell, New Jersey, to the pediatrician's office in Northfield. Bill came in his company car from Newark.
I don't remember who tended our older four sons.

I missed the exit on the traffic circle and had to round it twice. Still,
I arrived on time; punctuality was paramount with this doctor.

And although he, too, was on time, he was extremely nervous. He
kept saying, "I don't know you very well." Finally he gave us the results
of recent hospital tests.

By this time, five months after Kenny's birth, Bill and I knew something was wrong. This baby didn't seem to feel pain. He never cried to
be fed or changed. He didn't nurse. After months of trying new formu-
las, cleaning up projectile vomiting, and emptying his bowels by insert-
ing a gloved finger in his rectum, we decided he had a digestive
malformation needing major surgery. Wrong—he had a different kind
of malformation, one that could never be corrected in any way—
Down's Syndrome.

All the way home, Vaughn Monroe seemed to keep singing on the
radio, "Red Roses for a Blue Lady." It always means bleak weather,
numb thoughts, and rounding and rounding that traffic circle.

Frequently after that day I would sit crying in the rocker, feeding
Kenny, willing the almond-shaped eyes to change. Sometimes I pretended they were belatedly rounding, but I knew nothing was happening for Kenny as it had with his four older brothers.

They were relieved to have Kenny home. They'd vigorously pro-
tested, "Mommy, get baby. Mommy, get baby," when I'd left Kenny at
the hospital for those tests. Will was now six, in kindergarten.

Doug was over four; Jerry was three; Ron was just past two. They eagerly held Kenny and offered toys.

My husband Bill's despair was not eased by learning that the hospital had added television and telephone charges to Kenny's bill.

At my next checkup the obstetrician asked how the baby was.

I said, "He can never be anything."

He looked shocked, perhaps sincerely.

After I explained, he said, "Well, usually the nursery staff picks it up, but I guess this time they didn't. And I certainly didn't notice anything."

I suddenly remembered his words the first time I'd visited his fancy Montclair, New Jersey, office. I'd been seven months pregnant and had just moved from Arizona. My neighbors had highly recommended him. When I'd said so, he'd preened a little. "Well, I pride myself on delivering a good baby."

Something had made me respond, "Of course, you can only deliver the baby who's there."

After a pause, he'd said he was Jewish and had just learned that the cafeteria in Montclair's Mountainside Hospital where I would deliver Kenny spread butter on the hamburger buns. He loved those hamburgers, but because Jews couldn't eat dairy products with beef, he'd have to give up the hamburgers.

That same February we learned the Kenny's-age baby of church friends had cerebral palsy. Unaware, both sets of parents had been comparing one handicapped baby's growth against the other's.

As soon as possible, we took Kenny for complete evaluations. Physicians and social workers told us to put him in an institution. One said, "He'll probably never walk or talk, he'll keep having sehim respiratory and other illnesses, and his death will be a blessing." Once Kenny became so ill I did call the police and doctor to ask, "What do I do if someone dies in my home?" I can't remember what they said.

Repeatedly evaluators said that we needed to provide a normal life for our older children, that those boys had promise and needs that Kenny's problems would compromise. They predicted that we, especially I, would collapse under the burden of such a child.

Mother, who worked for the mental health department at a Salt Lake City hospital, asked the top doctor to evaluate Kenny. We'd come to Utah on vacation; our families now saw what Kenny was like. This doctor was even less encouraging than the New Jersey specialists. He told me, "You have a fine husband and normal children who need you and whom you need, unencumbered. Just as normal intelligence ranges, so does retardation, and Kenny is lowest in the low range. Don't hope."

Mother seemed relieved by the confirmation and began trying to enlist foster grandparents and other help for me in New Jersey.

Nothing came of it. Even children of our church friends were reluctant to babysit.

So we began visiting facilities for people like Kenny—and worse. Devastating—the deformities, the clutching, the babbling. Visiting battlefields would be less gruesome because I know many of those wounds heal.

We learned about costs, differences between private and state placement, and waiting lists. At home we boarded over the stair railings because Kenny would climb out and pose six feet up. He would let himself out of the house and run in the street. He would push his diapers off anywhere. He would pull things from tables or shelves. He climbed a bookcase and nearly pulled it over.

His brothers were tender with him. They knew he didn't wreck anything on purpose. When our oldest, Will, found his 1,000-piece jigsaw puzzle on the floor, he went rigid in rage. Then he picked up Kenny and took him upstairs to his crib. Had another brother been guilty, we would have had to call the paramedics.

In September 1972, a week before his fifth birthday, we and the state of New Jersey placed Kenny in Ann's Nursery in Norwalk, Connecticut. We paid a monthly fee calculated after deductions for taxes and other expenses, including those for our two sons with hearing losses and special shoes.

People soon said, "Carol, you're a different person, alive."

"You look years younger." I noticed it in Bill. Gradually, we realized that we could do nothing to help or hurt Kenny in this life, that professionals may be right about governments needing to help citizens with such burders. All we could do was visit regularly and pray he was cared for well and kindly.

As requested, we didn't visit Kenny for a month. He cried when we did. Will and Jerry, the brothers who could always comfort him, failed. I failed. Perhaps we confused him. Perhaps he could only remember people who cared for him daily.

Still, he was our child, and we needed to see how he was now and then. His brothers loved kicking autumn leaves over the lawns around the nursery, playing in the snow, and using the playground equipment. They loved the books and toys in the playroom.

But Kenny was too mobile and big; the facilities and programs weren't suitable for him. New Jersey officials soon found space in Keystone Residence in Burdens, Pennsylvania. But they said Bill and I had to transfer Kenny ourselves. We believed them then. My nightmares began. Always the same, the concern bringing Kenny home for a holiday during which a catastrophe keeps us from ever taking him back. I wake up sobbing.

Nevertheless, one Saturday in 1974 we packed our four older sons and a picnic lunch in our dark green Rambler station wagon and left home for what I expected to be a daytime nightmare. We would drive two hours to Connecticut, four to Burdens, and two back to West Caldwell. I prayed I could still feed Kenny the baby food I'd brought. I had always had to feed him first, alone. And if anything upset him, he would refuse to eat. Then only crawling into his crib would comfort him. I prayed he would nap in the back of the station wagon, or play, or at least not cry.

Amazingly, the trip went well. We made the usual picnic and play stops; the older boys seemed to have a great time. Kenny ate and slept, and at supper time we delivered him to Keystone. The several-storied building on a busy city street was as welcoming and well cared for as it had been on our previous visits. Staff members were thoughtful and reassuring.

Over the next few years, Kenny made progress, slowly. Almost a year passed before he could feed himself with a spoon. Toilet training took far longer and may not yet be complete. He suffered far less illness than before. We visited him once a month or so, trying merely to interact without causing tantrums. Naturally, his brothers played mainly with each other.

In 1976 we moved to Saudi Arabia. In 1978 we returned to New Jersey. In 1980 we moved to Utah. Kenny's placement was fine until we sold our New Jersey home and weren't taxpayers any more. New Jersey had already paid Connecticut and Pennsylvania for out-of-state care but would not let Utah pay in the same way. It would not let us leave Kenny where he was comfortable and progressing. We begged. No, officials said, we must move him.

Bill said, "No, if you want him moved, YOU move him."

He recalled that uneasy move from Connecticut to Pennsylvania. He was fed up with bureaucracy. He thought they were bluffing.

Regardless, he was firm. Financially and emotionally—I still have nightmares—we couldn't move Kenny this time.

Finally, the Keystone and New Jersey people arranged to fly Kenny to Salt Lake City. They said ticket money came from Kenny's Medicare or like account. I wonder—because for months afterward, we received from Keystone, supposedly for Kenny's clothing, bills that were old enough to have been paid from his account before his move. I was so angry I refused to respond.

Meanwhile, to find a place that would take Kenny, Bill and I visited Utah State Social Services offices many times and filled out many papers. We visited some facilities. Finally we chose West Jordan Care Center and made arrangements. It was a one-story residence, secure, well kept up, seemingly well-staffed. Kenny would share a room.

The date was set for the care center supervisor to meet us and Kenny at Salt Lake International Airport. Bill had to go to work but said he would meet me at the airport. Mother said, "You're not going alone. Pick me up on your way."

Our extremely concerned son, Ron, cut school or work, I don't remember which, to go with me. I kept wiping tears; I hoped I would be able to recognize the care center director.

"I'll drive, Mom," Ron said.

"Thanks, but I'm fine. You can drive home, though," I added, remembering he'd been the last to get a license and didn't have many chances to drive.

At the terminal we three walked to the designated gate and waited for arriving passengers to file by. Bill wasn't there. Neither was the care center director.

Finally from the plane came a blonde woman holding Kenny by the hand. She introduced herself as a social worker. I don't remember her name just her navy suit and flashy scarf and that Kenny was in a sweat-suit that he'd wet. She said she hadn't had any clothes to change him into. Considering her profession and that situation, I still can't imagine why.

Speaking to him, I took Kenny's other hand. We started down the concourse to baggage claim. Mother and Ron walked beside me.

The care center director ran up. "I'm so sorry. I was stuck in traffic."

Mother looked skeptical, then relieved. I mentioned the wet clothes. The director looked at the social worker. She said, "Well, I have to get the next plane back."

So we left the airport. I think we gathered Kenny's bags and went out to help him get into the care center director's car.

Before I could think of following along to the care center, Mother said, "You're not going home hungry. I'm taking you both to lunch at Sizzler."

Ron looked at his watch. I think he wanted to try to catch his later class at the university. But because his father had never appeared, he decided against letting me drive home alone.

We ate well at Sizzler; I loaded up on the salad bar as usual. We talked of many things, including Kenny. We had already prayed together that he would be all right.

Of course someone could physically injure Kenny; a subsequent social worker told me he suspects past abuse. And maybe someone could impede the progress even of one already so mentally and physically stunted. Bill, whose work had stalled everywhere all day, burst into tears when he finally got home and learned we'd coped.

And Kenny had to move again within a year. West Jordan personnel said he was too dangerous to himself and others. He would climb on others in their beds. He was also often sick—the change in climate, the doctors said.

"You'll have to take him home," officials told us.

"No, we don't have to take him home," Bill said. "He's a ward of the state of Utah. Now you say you have papers we need to sign, and we will sign them, to help transfer Kenny to another facility. But we do not have to take him home, and you know it."

So Kenny went to what was once called the Training School and is now the Development Center in American Fork. He lived in Quail

Run unit, and we got reports about his progress. Sometimes we attended a meeting about plans for his future training. We received forms to be signed by those who take relatives home for Thanksgiving, birthdays, Christmas. We began to get letters as if Kenny were writing to tell "Mom and Dad about the neat activities I am doing." I thanked them for the news but said, "Please don't pretend to be Kenny actually writing." They seemed offended.

Kenny has since had several operations and sometimes wears glasses. Dentists have to anesthetize him even to clean his teeth. Bill always went to the clinic or hospital to sign papers. Yet I was listed as the "responsible party" and received all the forms.

About ten years ago, we were asked to meet to review Kenny's candidacy for living in a group home. It was the only time questioners hadn't started by asking how old I had been when carrying Kenny, whether the pregnancy had been normal, and what my feelings had been. Kenny was present. I could restrain him by holding him with both hands and bracing myself.

The panel asked about Kenny's progress. I said they knew better than I. They asked my opinion about Kenny's placement in the group home. I asked what abilities and cognition such residents need to have. They told me. I asked if they thought Kenny had them. They said no. I said, "We're all wasting our time."

In June 1989 we were invited to Kenny's high school graduation. The state has to try to teach them until they reach age twenty-two. Bill had to work. My father (my mother had recently died) would not let me go alone. It was very hard to see Kenny wear a cap and gown and know it could not signify what it does for normal people. It was very hard to restrain him while we waited to have pictures taken. He was young teen height and nearly stronger than I. Dad, seventy-nine, suffering from shingles and a strained back, could not help.

Our experience and feelings are ambivalent. From the beginning, we had been counseled to write Kenny out of our wills and trusts and never to assume guardianship for him. Apparently the reason is that when we die, the state retains responsibility for Kenny. At the same time, those institutions have insisted that we assume responsibility for him. For years they requested information about getting Kenny on our medical insurance plans. We hadn't any. And they kept asking for data only they could know.

Dad continued to send birthday and Christmas cash for Kenny. We learned that if we gave more than $20 in a quarter, the state confiscated it. His picture remains in our living room. Grandchildren know his name. I used to include his news in letters.

None of our family or friends ever criticized us. We're more fortunate than a woman in our present church area who was scorned and ridiculed for placing her son in state care. Under pressure, she brought him home—and nearly lost her health—before placing him again. She nearly collapsed as a church speaker later enthused about the rewards of caring for a "special" child at home. Afterward I said to the visitor, "Three of us here have been unable to care for such children at home. In future talks consider mentioning that not all situations are alike—as fortunate as yours."

"No," she returned. "It was the greatest blessing."

A church official's talk in a subsequent general conference talk followed much the same line.

Two years ago the group home question came up again—under what pressures to mainstream more handicapped citizens I don't know. We were surveyed about Kenny's participation. We said we didn't think he was qualified. Somebody did. We were ultimately given a contact name and phone number for his new location in Bountiful, Utah. We haven't received any letters, though.

In 1997, when our son, Ron, and his wife, Loree, were getting help for their autistic-tendency son, Ron told a social worker that he doesn't even know where his Down's Syndrome brother is. Ron said we parents didn't knew, either. The social worker was appalled, said, "Give me his birthdate and name, and I'll find out. You have a right to know that!"

Near Christmas 1997 I sat with a cousin and her husband at a fundraiser. The husband, who works for a firm that does programs for people like Kenny, said, "Well, today they asked us to run some address labels for our clients, and your name was on the list. I hadn't realized that Kenny was yours."

I swallowed, "Well, how is he doing?

"Not much, not really well." My cousin-in-law shrugged.

"I know we can't expect much, but—" I remembered how his skin had cracked and bled in this dry climate. I told about the states that didn't care about anyone or anything but their tax rolls.

"His age may have been the factor. We've just placed a young woman in a facility in St. George, Utah, so she can be nearer her parents who moved to Las Vegas. She's past her majority."

I thought of our second son, Doug's, recent remarks. "You should be glad you have Kenny. You have it made with him. He can't give you any trouble. It's the rest of us boys you have to worry about."

Well, we'll see when we get the letter.

What Nobody Told Me

Jan Stucki

THEY TOLD ME EVERYTHING ELSE: that some days I would hold my baby and cry all afternoon, that for no reason I would get up in the night to listen to her breathe, that I would not mind the stink of my own baby's diapers. Who were they to know what I would do or feel? It bothered me that in their photocopied Christmas letters they all seemed to be raising the same child: our little two-year-old sure keeps us running. What happened to the intimate individuality of the parent-child bond? No, what really bothered me was that they were right. I can sit and watch her breathing all night long.

What nobody told me is that having a baby is like having a lover. I don't have any other words for this. But here are the facts: when I'm not with my baby, she's all I think about. I think about the last time we made eye contact and what it meant. Does she really like me? Does she think about me too? Is she squeezing my hand out of true affection or just as a passive reflex? And if there were one thing I could ask my little sweetheart, it would be that one annoying question reserved for lovers: So, what are you thinking?

I really mean this. It took so long for her to smile at me, or to give any indication that she knew who I was. All I wanted was for her to notice me and for two months she looked right through me.

These feelings—the obsession, the broken-hearted longing—I have known only in the context of romance. When she was four weeks old, my husband and I were given tickets to a concert I really wanted to see. It was the first time I'd left her and I needed to get out. I was half dead from the exhaustion of my constant fear that I would break her. But the whole time out, I thought of nothing but her pretty eyes, and looking back, the only thing I remember about the concert is the p.a. system playing "Wichita Lineman" when it was time to go get her. The last time a person distracted me that way I was fifteen and had a bad crush on Bruce Goodman. I never had a chance with Bruce Goodman, but I had a whole notebook full of "Mrs. Jan Goodman" written in every loopy style of cursive my hand could invent.

I know I'm not the first person to consider my relationship with my tiny baby to be romantic. My husband too picked her up one day and said, "You just want to have her hands on you, and your hands on her." And every baby book in print warns us to be prepared for the jealousy of dealing with our spouse's attachment to her. *What to Expect When You're Expecting* puts it in terms of the mother's jealousy of baby and father: "As harmless—even as heartwarming—as a budding romance between father and infant may seem to an outsider, it can be genuinely threatening to a woman who's not used to sharing her husband's affection, particularly if she's enjoyed his solicitous attention during nine months of pregnancy." Maybe. But I think we're more jealous of her attention than of each other's. He envies the comfort I can give her through breast feeding. What irks me is that she won't breast feed at all—or even look at me—when he's in the room. She pulls away from my nipple and strains about to stare at him.

On the other hand, whether or not we are used to describing our relationships with our babies in terms of romance, we are all very used to the way romantic relationships are described in the language of babies: "Baby, I need your lovin'." After all, cupid is an infant.

All of this is sweet. Our romance, though, is physical. It's more than just my neurotic emotional attachment. The urge to kiss her never stops. I love to feel her skin against mine, to hold her little naked body from head to toe against me. I love to take a bath with her and slide handfuls of water down her back. Most afternoons I let her roll around naked on the floor while I sit back and admire her little bum.

And she's physical with me, too. When I kiss her, she tries to stick her tongue in my mouth. When I hold her up to my face, she wants to suck on my nose. The other day when we were breast feeding she slid her hand under my shirt and pressed it warm against the curve of my ribs. It felt big and warm on my skin, like the hand of her father. She rubbed it up and down. And sometimes when she breast feeds, she stops and looks around and just licks at my nipple. Then after a while she sucks again. My husband jokes that when she is thirteen and mad at us he will tell her about this—the joke of course being that the licking of nipples seems so sexual that you don't even have to say how embarrassing it will be for her.

That's when the word "erotic" first came to mind. When I realized there was something between us that I was not entirely comfortable with. The first week I had her, I looked down at my tiny baby nursing at my breast—me hoping to look as much as possible like a soft-focus television commercial: innocent mother in white nightgown and hair ribboned back smiling down at innocent nursing baby also in white nightgown, spring breeze rippling the white gauze curtains near the bassinet—and I couldn't help but feel strange about it. She is sucking on my breast. And we both are liking it. Is this okay?

Our society sends us messages that it is not okay. I heard of a woman who breast fed for three years because she liked it, and then was reported to Child Protective Services the minute she said so. Our images of motherhood are ironically some of the most unsexual images in our culture (and virginity the most sexual). But when we say we enjoy breast feeding, we acknowledge the deep sensuality of this skin-to-skin contact. And in our culture sensuality is usually equated with sexuality. And sex is so terribly nasty. So sex in the context of breast feeding is especially perverse. The State of Utah just passed a law stating that breast feeding in public is *not* lewd behavior. Apparently a (female) store security guard had ripped the blanket off a nursing woman's shoulder and said, "I know what you're doing under there!" What I had hoped would be a wonderful experience was also tinged with scandal.

But isn't there such a thing as sexuality in absence of a desire to have sex? A sexuality that does not desire an illicit relationship on the floor of the back office? It seems to me that there is an intimate contact we have with our families that is good and healthy, innocent in its intimacy. There is a way we touch one another that is not nasty, and is still physically pleasurable.

I think it was more than pleasure, though, that made me feel strange about breast feeding. The other day my best friend told me about how, when she patted the naked bottom of her four-year-old daughter getting out of the tub, her daughter said, "Mom! You're not supposed to touch people's private parts!" When my friend told this story at the poker table, we all laughed and said that there was a childhood abuse story just waiting to be remembered in psychotherapy. Because when she said the words out loud—which accurately describe the action— the words "touch people's private parts" placed the caress of a mother in the same dangerous territory as the touch of a trenchcoated stranger. Just this morning I wrote in my journal that my baby had been chewing on my nose. Writing "chew" seemed to be the necessary restraint to make that action a safe one. But she wasn't chewing, she was sucking. The way she sucks on my nipple. It's just that "suck" can sound like such a nasty word.

That's what's really happening here: language. Sometimes I think it must have been the sound of the words used to talk about it—nipples, breasts, sucking—that kept so many women in the 1950s from breast feeding. Because even appropriate behavior can sound bad when spoken aloud. We are verbal animals, though, and our actions exist in language. And the language we use to describe our bodies has been eroticized. So, while there may be a continuum of sexual behavior— from safe and appropriate to dangerous and perverse—it is all talked about using the same language of the dangerous and perverse.

I sat there that first week nursing my baby, growing angry with my culture for having eroticized my breasts. The real problem, though, is not that body parts are eroticized, it's that the language is. So as innocent as your little baby may be when licking your nipples, the moment you put lick and nipple into the same sentence, you get sex, nasty and dangerous. But if you have a baby you have to use the words: lick, suck, nipple, tongue, boob, bum, and tup.

"Tup" was the word in my mother's family. Every family has them: the words we invent to disguise the sexuality of bodies. It means vagina. In our house it was used mostly in the context of little girls and bath time, as in "Did you get your tup clean?" I grew up thinking that this was just another family word—part of the wonderful private vocabulary of my mother's family—and that nobody unrelated to me had ever spoken it.

It was when we first took our girl to see my mother's family in St. George that my husband first heard it. I had honestly forgotten about it for a while. So when I was changing her diaper in the front room and my aunt said, "Ohhh, little tuppy tup," he thought she was being vulgar. When we got home, he showed me where he knew the word. In the first scene of *Othello,* Iago tells Brabantio that Othello is having sex with his daughter with the lines, "Even now, now, very now, an old black ram is tupping your white ewe." And the dictionary agreed. A tup is a ram (noun), but also a verb: "to copulate with." Had the whole world except my sister and me known this was a sexual slur?

My southern Utah farmer ancestors who said tup a hundred years ago may or may not have known what they were talking about. But for a city girl like me, the language that I had come to see as invented to protect me from my own sexuality was in truth an unwitting mockery of it.

I think now that, although we can pretend, there is no escaping the sexuality of the language that we use to describe our bodies. The fact that we would invent words to hide the names of those body parts is already an indication that we are covering something dirty. And I'm not certain I would want to escape this phenomenon. That is, if sometimes innocent actions sound nasty because of the way they appear in our eroticized language of bodies, then a less eroticized language might permit perverse actions to be described as innocent. There are reasons we police our language.

The reason nobody told me that having a baby is erotic, I imagine, is that to say the words aloud is to come too close to a perverse relationship we don't want to have with our children. And the truth is, that now that my baby is five months old, breast feeding is not so novel and I am less often trying to translate all her actions into language in my head. So I am less concerned with how our body parts rub against each other in sentences. But I can't deny that what I love about having a baby is the comforting physical intimacy that is similar to, but different from, the intimacy I have with my husband. And that the difference is difficult to express.

Among Linens

Lara Candland

I go to the closet
unfold a linen
comfort my baby
inconsolable girl.

You sleep. In the morning
you wake but I'm still in bed
and I weep. Her little teeth
lost bottle,
my large body.

Sweet, salty—
I eat like this
all day, this
rhythmically
at night I stop
then start again
by lifting a lasagne
from the oven.

Sweet, salty
baby sleeps
among linens.

Once young
I slept, I wept
for you.

Little Apples

Lara Candland

in tiny girl hand
swiftness of motion
pitch of voice
cheeks of girl
are fabrics
beheld
in awe

girl running
speaks a new word
shalt not hear
my call but continue
moving
my fruit
little apple
the imbricate inlay
of the two skins
touching

Loss

Death and Life

Francine Bennion

THREE TIMES MY DOCTOR declared me dead at the birth of my first baby.

My husband, Bob, and I were both in graduate school at Ohio State University, married for three months, when I became pregnant in December 1956. I had no nausea, felt good though sleepy at times, and found it easier than ever in my life to eat exactly as I should, because I was doing it for the baby.

When I was about six months along, I had some blood spotting, and at nearly seven months a little bright bleeding. My obstetrician told us that the placenta was over the opening of the uterus, and hemorrhaging was possible at any time.

Bob was working and training five days a week at the Veterans Administration hospital in Chillicothe, an hour away from our upstairs apartment in Columbus. Our widowed landlady, old and quite deaf, had neither a car nor any experience driving one. Downstairs in her dining room, the receiver, coated with fragrant layers of spittle because her false teeth fit badly, was the only phone in the house, and we had to ask her permission to use it. Our friends lived on narrow streets in other parts of town, and there was no close help for an emergency. We agreed that I should fly home to Lethbridge, Alberta, Canada, where I could be with my parents.

My father met me at the nearest convenient airport, in Great Falls, Montana. He was alone. My mother had gone up to the small Ukrainian town in northern Alberta where my sister Rosemary lived with her physician husband and four young daughters. Rosemary was in the hospital. Days of hard ineffectual labor had ended in the birth of a purple girl weighing more than nine pounds who died within hours of

163

birth. She was given my name.

A week later Dad and I went to a movie. When we got home about 9:30 that evening, I felt some pressure and went into the bathroom. A sudden astonishing flood of warm bright blood fell out and kept coming. And coming. All over my legs, my clothes, all over the floor. How could there be any left? "Dad. Dad."

I couldn't walk right. Dad helped me to bed, and I worried that he would have to clean up the mess alone—all over the sheets and mattress, a stream, a red river.

My white-faced father went to the phone and called Dr. Fowler, a founder of the medical clinic my father managed, our family doctor all the years I was growing up, the doctor who gave me ether and sewed up the cut under my nose when I fell off a basketball on which I was trying to balance like a seal when I was five years old.

"What did he say?"

"He said he is just leaving to find his horse that's lost on The Reservation. He said to stay in bed and he'll come and check you when he gets back."

Dad sat on a chair by the bed. I bled steadily, though less copiously, and at times Dad would put another fresh Hudson Bay wool blanket under me to absorb the blood. I lay frozen, tense, afraid to move for fear of precipitating a catastrophe. After a while my legs began to tremble. I couldn't get them to stop. "Dad. My legs won't stop shaking. And it's hard to talk because my jaw is shaking too. My teeth are chattering."

Dad phoned another doctor in the clinic, Dr. Poulsen, whose daughter was the friend with whom I used to roller skate, and hike in the river bottom to Six Mile Coulee. Dr. Poulsen came and gave me a shot that was supposed to stop the shaking and the contractions I was beginning to have. He stayed a while, then said to call the ambulance if things didn't calm down within an hour or two, or if I began bleeding more heavily again. I was Dr. Fowler's patient, and Dr. Fowler was expected back any minute. Dr. Poulsen would not interfere.

I continued trembling and contracting, and the bleeding accelerated, sometimes coming in warm surges. At midnight I was carried to the ambulance and put in a private room at the hospital. Saying it would be best if I tried to sleep, the night nurse sent Dad home. She would call him as soon as the doctor came.

My memory of what followed is fuzzy, more in my body than in my head. Focusing now for the first time in years, I discover the memory of those long hours in my legs, my abdomen, my pelvis, my still arms and shoulders. I haven't words for the long dark night, warm blood flowing, labor contractions, in the dark alone and afraid to move or turn over, weak, numb, legs still trembling. Can the baby live? I had thought of her as Susan. I had eaten for her, welcomed her kicks, waited for her.

At long intervals the nurse would come to change soaked pads under me and put a stethoscope on the swollen belly I would have thought hollow after all the bleeding.

"What can you hear?"

"There's a heartbeat."

The baby was alive at 2:00 a.m., and the doctor had not come.

"What can you hear?"

"There's a heartbeat."

The baby was alive at 4:00 a.m., and the doctor had not come.

"What can you hear?"

"I'm not sure."

And again, later, "What can you hear?"

"I'm not sure."

Now I cry, writing this. I didn't then. Unspeakably tired, reason and emotion pale, hope for the baby faint, I lay on warm blood, letting happen what would.

At 6:30 a.m. Dr. Fowler came to the hospital, after retrieving his horse. He scrubbed, and I was taken to the delivery room too weak for anesthetic, too weak to give my baby birth, too much blood gone to survive surgery.

What I remember now, and what I experienced then, is dim, distant, muffled. Again, as I try to remember, I feel my body change.

I heard someone say there was no heartbeat for the baby. The nurses' uncertainty had told me that, but I had still hoped.

I knew there was light, but I could no longer open my eyes. I could hear people murmuring and moving, but I could not tell what they were doing. I heard the doctor say, "She has no pulse, she has no breath," heard him from a distance say, "I'll go in and take it," after a while felt the slightest pressure again on my wrist, heard him say, "She's gone," felt an agony of intrusion as he inserted forceps into my uterus and pulled, then felt nothing. Again he said, "She's gone," this time his voice faint and moving away.

I wasn't gone. I wanted to say so. I couldn't speak or move but I was there, however distant and unseeing, and I could hear him. I thought of Bob, and how he would be if I did not return to him, what he would do if he knew I had gone home and died. I didn't care where I was, I was so tired, so far and tired, but I could not leave Bob alone.

I thought the baby was a girl, but I couldn't ask. I wanted to see eyes and fingernails and hair, wanted to know if there were the right number of fingers, but I couldn't speak. I knew people were moving across the room, and I was afraid they were putting my baby in a paper bag with other garbage in a can, but I couldn't protest. I could not move anything.

Then I was nowhere.

When I opened my eyes again, a tube was in my vein and Dad was there. I asked to see the baby. "They say it will be better if you don't." I was too tired to beg. I asked him not to let them throw her away but to find her and bury her in the cemetery. Later they did, in a white dress and a handkerchief for a diaper, in a grassy plot on which they put a small gravestone engraved "Baby Bennion." My mother says it was a beautiful little girl with lots of dark hair.

Dad phoned Bob. He was at the VA hospital in Chillicothe as usual that day, playing baseball out on the lawn with other trainees and staff in honor of some special celebration. He was called in to answer the phone in the hall, but couldn't hear very well because of the noise and confusion around him.

"Bob?"

"Yes."

"This is Fran."

"Who?"

"Fran."

Bob couldn't hear. "Who?"

"Fran. Francine's Dad."

Bob thought he said, "Francine's dead."

Early on I had asked Dad to put me in a ward instead of a private room, not telling him it was to save money. I went to sleep with blood pumping into me, and woke up in an eight-bed ward, still hooked up to a bottle. That day I was given all the compatible blood the hospital had, five pints. In the week that followed, I was given four more pints.

The women in all the other beds had babies. On schedule, their babies were wheeled in for the mothers to feed them, coo to them, love them. That was all right. I was glad for them.

But then my milk came in. The doctor had prescribed pills to prevent it, but they didn't work. I was swollen from my waist to my collarbone, not only my breasts but my whole chest rock hard, an agonizing unyielding mass of tissue with milk pushing to burst my skin. I begged for help. "We can pump it," they said, "but that will only keep the milk coming and prolong your discomfort." Discomfort.

One night when the babies were brought in at 2:00 a.m., I lay sleepless, watching in pain, aching for a baby to drain me of that unbearable milk in softness and love, yearning for Bob to hug me. I waited till the feeding was over and babies taken away, lights turned off, hallways quiet, mothers sleeping. Then I awkwardly eased out of bed and in slow stiff agony walked the dark halls, turning back again and again to avoid the lighted nurse's station, tears streaming my cheeks and my stone chest.

Finally I dabbed my face with the sleeve of my printed cotton gown and made my way to the nurse at the desk. "My chest hurts," I managed to say, quite politely. "Can you give me something for pain?" She consulted my chart. "Nothing is ordered." Then she looked at my face. "I think it would be all right if I give you a couple of aspirin."

Gratefully I swallowed the pills and the water, walked back in the direction of the ward as though returning to bed, and lumbered in dark silence again. Later the nurse came to check on me, found me around a hall corner, and took me to bed.

After some days my blood count became closer to normal, and though my chest still hurt, it was a little less tight because milk was leaking. With bands of washable cotton bound tightly around my breasts, I went home to my mother and father.

The milk kept coming. I remember going to a bridal shower weeks later for Iris Kirk, who had become a pharmacist and had given me crystal goblets for my wedding. Though I was still white and tired, I wanted Iris to know I was her friend. I don't remember much about the shower except that when it was time to leave, I felt something wet and looked down to find the front of my tan linen dress soaked with milk.

A well-meaning woman phoned to comfort me with promises that I would raise my baby in the next world. As she talked, I remembered riding to summer school at Brigham Young University years before. The man sitting next to me on the bus, a Mormon high priest from Raymond, had asked if I knew when the spirit enters a baby's body. "No," I said, and he told me the true answer with satisfaction, quoting a scripture from the Book of Mormon to prove he was right. I thought of a New Testament scripture that seemed to contradict his, but I really didn't care and didn't feel like arguing because it seemed fruitless. Now his question was perhaps more pertinent, but after thanking the caller and hanging up, I could not pretend to know any more than I had when I was younger, or to find argument from limited resources more fruitful. I was only human. Raising a "baby" in the next life did not make sense to me.

My hemorrhage was real. My God was, and is, real. Speculative hopes were not my rock, my ground.

I wrote a letter to the English department at Ohio State asking if they needed me to teach composition, logic, and literature fall term. I received a quick reply offering me a position.

At the end of August I returned to Columbus and normal life, walking a couple of miles with Bob to campus, continuing graduate studies, cooking, making music at church, doing laundry in a portable machine in the bathtub in case the water leaked, watching Bob's foot go through our living-room floor and the ceiling below one day as he walked toward the kitchen, teaching a cynical Korean veteran, fraternity and sorority pledges, farm girls, and a nonchalant from the slums of Cleveland, shopping for groceries and encountering chocolate-covered ants and canned rattlesnake meat in the gourmet section at Big Bear, where one of our impoverished student friends was in the habit of intercepting overripe bananas and browning lettuce headed for the garbage bins ...

When Bob finally learned that Dr. Fowler had gone to look for his horse while I lay bleeding, and Dr. Poulsen had feared Dr. Fowler more than my death, he raged at the men, and would have been after them with a crowbar. I thought them only human.

My long bloody night with death was past. It became a half-remembered dream, distant from fallen buckeyes, bright cardinals, quiet snow. I awoke Christmas morning liking the light slanting through our bedroom window, and wrote a card to Dr. Fowler thanking him for saving my life.

The following year the first of our lively children was born.

Spencer Roy Barentsen

Kim Barentsen

I AM A CHILDLESS MOTHER. ONE month ago my first child, Spencer, was born dead after seven months of pregnancy. I feel as though I will never recover from the pain of missing him, or understand why he had to leave me. The whole experience seems incongruous— pregnancy is about life, not death.

I loved my son deeply. From the beginning, when I threw up three times a day, to the last few strong kicks that I felt at the end, he was my darling little boy. My husband and I read him stories in utero, and I could tell he liked them, especially "Goodnight Moon," as I did as a child. While showering, lying in bed at night, at all times of the day, I rubbed my protruding tummy and encouraged him to grow strong. I talked to him, about ideas, about how I was feeling. I drank pink lemonade Snapple, ate dill pickles, couldn't eat enough oranges to satisfy him. While driving in the car, I always made sure classical music was playing to heighten his development. I subscribed to every parenting magazine available.

I pictured myself as a proud mom this summer, pushing him in the new stroller I bought, showing him off. I longed to hear him cry. More than anything, I couldn't wait to hear him call me "Mommy." Even now, whenever I hear a child call his mother "Mommy," I tear up, wondering if someone will ever call me by that name.

Oh, how I long to be a mother! I've never wanted anything more in my entire life. My arms are empty, and they ache to hold him. I am obsessed with getting pregnant again. As much as I want it though, I am afraid. I will never rest easy. What if the same thing happens again? At times I feel that I am not like other people. I'm jealous of other women who effortlessly have healthy babies. I have failed at the most important thing in my life, and I'm scared I'll never be able to carry a live baby to term, to hear it cry. Writing that statement makes me shudder as I realize how deeply I feel that fear. But I must go on. I have to try again.

I wasn't always so obsessed with motherhood. In fact, I have never wanted those things that are part of being a traditional Mormon woman. After I went on a mission to Hong Kong and graduated from Brigham Young University, I moved to San Francisco and worked as an investment consultant at a major bank. Every year I doubled my income and moved higher and higher up the ranking sheets as a "top producer." I was validated by my big career, part of me was frightened to be a mother and lose that part of myself.

Life was good for my husband and me. We were having fun being married, travelling up and down the coast of California every other weekend. My co-workers, who thought I was too young to get married at twenty-five, definitely thought that I should wait to have children until I was much older. But I realized that there was more to life than a demanding career. We gave up birth control and tried to get pregnant for about a year. When the home pregnancy test finally showed a positive sign, I was thrilled. Scott and I jumped around, hugging each other and laughing. As inadequately prepared as I felt, I was very happy

I'm terrified that I killed my baby. Now, in some of my darker moments, I imagine that having my career for so long, waiting to have a baby, these things caused Spencer's death. Maybe it was unresolved sins in my past. He was living inside of me, supported by my body and my breath. I've blamed secondhand smoke, being out of shape, not attending the temple enough, or drinking Diet Coke while I was pregnant. Maybe it happened while my husband and I made love the weekend before we found out that the baby was dead. Some well-meaning people have suggested that my severe morning sickness was the problem. Others blame the stress that I experienced from my job. I'm sure I'll think of more ways to blame myself because it all seems completely beyond my control. I struggle to deal with problems with no cause. It makes little difference what my doctor says. She says it was a fluke, nothing that I did caused it to happen. Some days I believe her, some I don't.

I need to know exactly what happened to Spencer. I am so scared that he suffered, that I starved him to death. I'll probably never know, but I hope that he didn't feel any pain, that his spirit was taken long before his eventual physical demise. The autopsy showed that the cord was attached poorly, and the placenta was malformed and abrupted in one spot. Other than that, we really don't know why—the baby was perfect, no genetic problems. Placental problems rarely recur, but then only about a million other things can go wrong in pregnancy. I know, because I've read about them all. I continue to read medical journals and own over ten books on stillbirth. I need to know that this has happened to other people, not just me. Every time I read or hear the story of a woman having living children after this experience, I feel a tug on my heart. Maybe, just maybe, that will be me.

My pregnancy was not routine. I had severe morning sickness that kept me out of work from the eighth week on. Our ten-week ultrasound was accurate with my dates, but the twenty-week showed that he was only eighteen weeks along. The perinatologist originally said that it was no big deal, they would just change my dates. But as they examined it further after the twenty-two-week ultrasound, he was even smaller. He kept falling farther and farther behind. Friends and family reassured us that he was just a small baby. The first indication of a problem came in mid-January, when my doctor called and told me that the original dates were accurate. I was relieved, but then she dropped a bomb. She strongly recommended an amniocentesis, as this kind of growth retardation is sometimes caused by chromosomal abnormalities. I hung up the phone and sobbed. Something might be wrong with our baby! The next day I called the doctor, ready to take my chances and not have the amnio. She insisted on the amnio, because the baby could be "incompatible with life."

I was terrified of the amniocentesis, of the giant needle. I was so worried about the baby being hurt. After the procedure I waited the longest two weeks of my life. Everyone close to us was fasting and praying. I thought that if he made it through the amnio all right we were home free. The answer came—"normal male fetus." I felt as if I'd won an olympic medal. I ordered a complete custom made nursery, arranged to have the baby furniture delivered, and finally relaxed. We celebrated with a romantic weekend in Napa. In eleven short weeks we would finally have a baby, after all these trials.

The next morning the sun shone, after weeks of rain. I had a routine office visit, and when I saw the doctor I gloated over the results of the amnio, like I'd passed some difficult test. I was chatting away about how happy I was when the doctor couldn't find a heartbeat with the Doppler. I still wasn't too worried, as I figured that the baby was hiding or her instrument was malfunctioning. I called my husband, and he met me at the perinatologist's office for another ultrasound. The technician couldn't find a heartbeat either. I made her check over and over again. She looked at me and flatly stated, "Your baby is dead."

I couldn't believe it was true, but my husband was weeping uncontrollably. I kept reassuring him that it would be okay. Our baby couldn't be dead. And if it really was true, I was honestly disgusted that I had a dead body inside of me. Could that be the same baby who kicked strongly, who was always there for me? All we could see on the ultrasound screen was the spine; the beating heart that I had taken for granted was gone. I kept going back to the amnio, and how happy I had felt that he was all right. I was in shock and denial. I knew that the baby was small, but what caused him to die? I clung to some desperate hope that he would be resuscitated, or that they were mistaken and his heart was still beating. I swore that sometimes I could still feel his little kicks inside of me.

For two days I continued with this hope. We went to the hospital, and after twelve hours of hard induced labor I delivered him. Through the entire labor I imagined that I would actually be delivering a live baby, that this was one of those "modern miracles" that people go on about in testimony meetings. I imagined calling my parents and telling them there was a mistake, that Spencer was a healthy baby boy. When I finally did push him out, he didn't cry, and I knew that my miracle wasn't going to happen. The realization hit me like a brick wall. I was scared to see his body, scared that I wouldn't love him.

I did love him though. From the moment I saw him, I fell in love as I never had before. Cradling him in my arms, I finally felt like a mother, at least for those few hours. He had a perfect little two-pound body, and his blue eyes were intense and beautiful. He had broad shoulders like his dad, and my nose and lips. Scott and I prayed, held him, and talked to him for several hours. I will always cherish that time with him. He was still our son, even though he was dead. We took pictures, and the nurses took his hand and foot prints. We felt his love for us, and ours for him. We felt God near. It was actually a spiritual experience and the veil was thin. We felt strongly impressed that we would have more children.

It broke my heart to leave the hospital without Spencer, alone. We came home to an empty house. Those first few days are still a blur to me. I cried continuously and took painkillers to numb myself into a few hours of fitful sleep. I wanted to sleep forever. I couldn't bear to look into the room we had prepared for him. Thinking about the future—the next day, the next week—was impossible. I couldn't watch television, read books or magazines. The world stopped for me when my son died. I was left to stare at the ceiling fan and mourn.

Immediately after this tragedy I felt very close to my husband. That emotional intimacy is indescribable. We had both been through a major crisis in the loss of our son, and I knew that he understood me like no other. But that closeness didn't last. A week after Spencer's death, Scott went back to work. I felt so alone. I still do. We are grieving very differently. Scott's approach to grief is to throw himself into his work. His absence has been hard on me and our marriage. We are arguing more often than ever before, over stupid things. We are both committed to our relationship, but I wonder how long this storm will last. I feel abandoned and alone. First I lost my son to death, and then my husband to his job. Every evening we pray together and we feel close. We hold hands and are intimate for those few minutes. We ask the Lord to bless our son and watch over him until we can be with him again, to give us peace. I suppose it's the stress of losing Spencer that causes us to argue. It astounds me that we can go from feeling so close at our daily prayers to arguing about unloading the dishwasher. Our moods continue to swing wildly. We are trying to communicate and understand each other, and we're slowly making progress.

Fortunately, my mom came out from Utah after this happened. She helped us with the necessary details. We suffered through a rude sales person at the cemetery, and an insensitive mortician. On top of dealing with our grief, we were forced to discuss cemeteries, plots, gravestones, caskets, ugly things I never imagined myself discussing for my child. "I am only twenty-eight, I'm not meant to deal with death!" I wanted to cry out at the mortuary. For them this was all in a day's work, but I had lost my only son! We didn't get much comfort from local church leaders, as there is no stated doctrine on stillborn children. We are encouraged to place his name on our family group sheet, to write that he was "born in the covenant." Our experience, though, has taught us that we will raise him later, after the resurrection. Bruce R. McConkie states that "It would appear that we can look forward with hope and anticipation for the resurrection of stillborn children." We are comforted by that statement, and we agree with him. We held a small graveside service for Spencer and sang "God Be with You 'till We Meet Again."

Time has passed slowly. I am still on disability from work, and unsure if I will ever go back to work at all. Two weeks after his death, I figured that returning to work was the answer, turning back the clock, going to a place where I'd been successful before. But in spite of my wish to act as though nothing ever happened, I know I cannot do that, I know that it's impossible. I am a changed person. I'm thinking about a master's degree at Berkeley, but more than anything I anticipate my children. I still cry almost every day, and I visit my son's grave daily and talk with him. I've prepared a box for him with his special things: a videotape of his ultrasounds, his bracelet from the hospital, his pictures, mementos from his pregnancy. I'm writing a series of entries in a book to him while I'm at the cemetery or at home thinking about him. There are things that I want to tell him. I want him to know who I am. I want to tell him about my life—my parents, my college experience, my mission, how I met and married his dad—he needs to know his mother. He also needs to know my impressions of him, my hopes for him. Above all, he absolutely needs to know how deeply I love him and how much I miss him. Every entry in the book resounds with this love.

Motherhood has changed my life. The power to help create life, nurture a child growing within, and raise that child amazes me. I'd taken it for granted. I never knew what an absolute miracle it is when a healthy baby is born. I know that we will be with Spencer again. For now I am Spencer's mother, and the short time that I spent with him will be with me forever. He will always be with me, and I will never stop loving him, for he is my firstborn son.

One More Long Poem

to eva

Lara Candland

You will imagine and imagine my face
and how its transience is now stilled.
You will see me to my box and have me covered
and surrounded.

I will be in my box and not in my box;
you will speak to me and not know if I hear.

As I do not now know but only imagine the fleeting brush
of ancestor's arm or the watchfulness of him,
you also will wish to be
but not know if you are watched.

That I will be in dirt and you will be
in air—we do not know if I am happy. We do not know
which visitors I receive. Take some comfort
in hoping that I have received Poe, or he me. Hope
that I am preparing to meet you again—*know*
that I will lift in time to carry you.
Take these words like they are my flesh
carved out and bled for you as I have always.

you are my flesh   remember me

Instructions for My Funeral
and Other Posthumous Thoughts

Louise Plummer

THE FUNERAL: It should be one hour exactly. No one's life is so interesting that it should be reviewed for longer than that. Don't allow
anyone to speak who does not know that one typed, double-spaced
page is two minutes of talking. Don't let anyone speak "from the
heart." It's one step above speaking in tongues. Have a thesis. Focus.
Only people with a strong sense of irony and language should be al-
lowed to speak.

Tell them that Tom and I danced in the kitchen to Les Brown and
his Band of Renown. Tell them I was called Loesje the first twenty years
of my life. Tell them I made needlepoint Christmas stockings for each
of my four sons. Tell them I was the Miata convertible grandma. Tell
them I once made a prayer tree. Tell them I beat Tom at Backgammon
55 percent of the time. Tell them I laughed a lot. Tell them I had a nice
alto/tenor voice. Tell them I loved the hymns and hated it when a
member of the bishopric would say at the end of sacrament meeting:
"Because of the time we'll only sing one verse." Some of us pray by singing. Tell them I could play "The Dance of the Blessed Spirits" on the
flute. Tell them I could draw Barney from memory. Tell them I could
curl my tongue.

Don't tell them about green bagging my son's bedroom. Don't tell
them about the burping contest in the HarMar parking lot. Don't tell
them about the time I stayed under the covers in my bed all evening because I thought I couldn't learn the Dutch passive voice and it was the
only thing standing between me and a master's degree. Don't tell them
how I repeatedly threatened to burn my study. Don't tell them about
the anxiety depressions. Don't tell them I had to take remedial math in

college.

You can quote me. I expect it.

THE VIEWING: Absolutely no open casket. I don't want people looking *down* at me. I don't want them saying, "She looks like she's sleeping." How would they know? I didn't sleep the last third of my life. I roamed the house, watched videos, and drank hot chocolate. When I'm dead, I'll look dead. Brown pancake make-up will cover the liver spots on my hands. Alive, I never made up my hands. I did make up my face, but Larkins won't get it right. They won't know that I wore L'Oreal's "Sandstone" lipstick and a suntan blush made by Dermablend. They won't wash my body with Chanel No. 5 soap like I did every morning. I won't smell right. Keep the casket closed.

And cover it with dozens of the palest pink roses. You can buy them at Hubbard's Floral on South Temple. At this writing they cost $4.50 apiece. Buy dozens. Spare no expense. I won't be asking again.

THE OBITUARY: Like the funeral, it should be of modest length. Don't write every minor accomplishment into it. It makes readers cynical. I was born. I went to school. I got married. I had children and grandchildren. I wrote a few books. I taught. I died. No phrasing like, "Our beloved wife, mother and grandmother has left this vale of tears," or "Heavenly Father took our beloved mother back to his bosom." And don't tell people that "in lieu of flowers" they can send a contribution to some charity. I want flowers. I want a roomful of flowers. (See above.)

THE BURIAL: The honest truth is that I would prefer to be cremated, but my family is so repelled by the idea of burning—as if being buried six feet in the ground is such a pleasure—that I doubt they could follow through with this. So my second choice is to be buried in the Salt Lake City cemetery where I enjoyed walking when I was a teenager. My sister, Joyce, is buried there. My grandparents are buried there. I want to be buried next to Tom. He is the first person I want to see on resurrection morning.

THE GRAVESTONE: I don't like gravestones that identify the relationship of the dead person to the one buying the gravestone, such as

"Mother" or "Beloved Wife." What if a grandchild comes to call? Or a friend? My name and the important dates are all that is needed.

THINGS I NEVER BELIEVED: (1) I never believed seminary was as important as real school. (2) I never believed Miss McCormack, my sixth grade teacher, when she said she'd muzzle me if I didn't stop talking. (3) I never believed that maxim, "Early to bed, Early to Rise, Makes a man happy, healthy, and wise." There are just as many hours in the day if you go to bed late and get up late. (4) I never believed Miss Bowman, my a cappella director, when she said that Barbra Streisand's voice wouldn't last, because she sang the wrong way. (5) I never believed people who said the best Christmas in their lives was the year they received an orange. (6) I never believed the people who told me that after marriage all the fun stops.

THINGS I BELIEVED: (1) I believed my father when he said hot dogs were made from dog tails. I was fifteen at the time. (2) I believed in Jesus. (3) I believed Mr. Bennett, my high school history teacher, when he said life just flies by after high school. (4) I believed Tom was magic. (5) I believed the patriarch when he said I would be satisfied with my life. (6) I believed the fortune cookie that said luck was with me now—act upon my instincts. (7) I believed I was a competent aesthetic advisor.

APOLOGIES TO MY FOUR SONS: I'm sorry I made you wear Sears Toughskins and, later, Oscar de la Renta jeans. Ed, I'm sorry you had to play hockey wearing my white figure skates. Charles, I'm sorry you had two spankings. I'm sorry I let Dad take your temperatures with a rectal thermometer. I know this has ruined your lives. Jon, I'm sorry you never got a skateboard for Christmas. Sam, I'm sorry I let your hair grow so long that people thought you were a girl. I'm sorry about the couscous with lamb and apricots, but that was Dad's doing. Remember, I'm the one who was easy with money and discipline, so get a grip.

APOLOGIES TO MY HUSBAND: Forgive me for making you sit through a Doris Day double-feature. I'm sorry that I was such a high-maintenance wife. Thank you for acting as though you never wanted anything else. We were good together, weren't we?

I hope I died before I became a mad, old woman, alone, wandering the streets of downtown Salt Lake wearing high-tops and a baseball cap. I'm pretty sure I'm headed for heaven. See you there.

For my sister, nearing armistice

Linda Sillitoe

You now are sentry, also army nurse,
deep in battle plans to blast the horde.
You also bore the battleground and the prize—
this dark-eyed girl who, at three, won four and five.
Outside her hospital window, spring gains force,
spurting dandelions through bricks and boards,
loading birds in trees as pollen swirls the skies.
In all that life, where's one for her to live?

If the needles stabbed, the chemicals all failed,
and her hair drifted from her clever head like all
your questions (prayers) scouting the nights,
still, each dawn you woke with her and smiled.

Now trust each cup you lift to soothe like rainfall,
for bending toward her, you are rimmed with light.

Contributors

ILA ASPLUND is a soon-to-be graduate of the University of Washington in Seattle. She will finish her university studies abroad in Indonesia, where she will continue to work on her poetry as well as study the art of batik. Ila is interested in the combination of visual art and text; her journals are filled with observations in both words and images.

MARNI ASPLUND-CAMPBELL lives, teaches English, and writes in Seattle, Washington, with her three children and husband, Greg.

KIM BARENTSEN holds a B.S. degree in psychology with honors from Brigham Young University. She is the mother of Spencer and a charming two-year-old boy, David John. Kim is a stay-at-home mom who works part time out of her house as a licensed stockbroker and investment consultant. She and her family reside in the San Francisco Bay area.

FRANCINE BENNION was born in Lethbridge, Alberta, Canada, in 1935. She and her husband, Robert, have a daughter, Lynne, two sons, Roald and Brett, and four grandchildren. Francine holds degrees in music, French, and English and taught part time for twenty-five years at Ohio State University and Brigham Young University, retiring in 1997 after seven years of team-teaching Honors History of Civilization with her husband. She is glad to be alive.

MARION BISHOP has degrees in English literature, rhetoric, and composition from New York University and Utah State University. Her doctoral research focused on how women use diaries to name and construct their lives. In addition to her academic publications, she has published a personal essay in *Dialogue: A Journal of Mormon Thought*. She teaches at Bentley College in Waltham, Massachusetts.

ELIZABETH BRADLEY graduated from Pacific University, in Oregon, in creative writing. She is the mother of Aspen Elizabeth Bradley.

MARTHA SONNTAG BRADLEY teaches at the University of Utah and is co-editor of *Dialogue: A Journal of Mormon Thought.*

PANDORA BREWER has lived in Cambridge, Massachusetts, for the past ten years. She has also lived in other states and in Japan. She has a husband working on his dissertation at Harvard, and two small boys. She works as a retail manager. She teaches Sunday school and fears death.

JOANNA BROOKS is a fourth-generation Los Angeleno, the descendent of Okies, Basque Californios, and handcart pioneers. Her poetry, fiction, and academic writing have been published in a number of journals and anthologies. She is currently completing a Ph.D. in American literature at the University of California, Los Angeles.

ARLENE BURRASTON-WHITE was born and raised in Utah. She is the mother of three and grandmother of one. A free-lance writer and editor, she currently resides in Virginia with her husband, O. Kendall White, Jr.

LYNN CLARK CALLISTER, R.N., Ph.D., is assistant dean as well as an Assistant Professor in the College of Nursing at Brigham Young University.

LARA CANDLAND is poetry editor for *HipMama* magazine. She has published poetry and fiction in many journals and anthologies, including *The Quarterly* and *Bite to Eat Place.* She is the co-founder of Seattle Experimental Opera and is its chief librettist.

KARIN ENGLAND lives in Alpine, Utah. She is in the creative writing Ph.D. program at the University of Utah and is a member of the English faculty at Utah Valley State College.

KAREN FARB lives and works in New York with her son, Ian.

SUSAN ELIZABETH HOWE is an associate professor of English at Brigham Young University, Provo, Utah. She is the poetry editor of *Dialogue: A Journal of Mormon Thought* and has also been the poetry editor of *Exponent II* and the managing editor of *The Denver Quarterly*. The poem "Fighting with My Mother" is from her first collection, *Stone Spirits,* which was published in 1997 by the Charles Redd Center for Western Studies.

EILEEN GIBBONS KUMP lives in St. Joseph, Missouri. "Bread and Milk" appears in her collection of short stories entitled *Bread and Milk*.

JULIE NICHOLS is a part-time instructor of creative writing at Brigham Young University, has a husband and four children (one on a mission in Venezuela), and is currently at work on a book describing her experiences as an apprentice at Touchstone, a healing and educating center in Cotati, California.

DIXIE LEE PARTRIDGE grew up in Wyoming on a farm homesteaded by her great-grandfather. Her first book, *Deer in the Haystacks* (1984), is part of the Ahsahta Press series Poetry of the West. Her second, *Watermark* (Saturday Press, 1991), won a national Eileen Barnes Award. She is working on her fourth collection, and looking for a publisher for her third, *Not About Dreams*. Her poetry and essays have appeared widely in such journals as *The Georgia Review, Commonweal, Midwest Quarterly, Northern Lights, Ploughshares, Southern Poetry Review, Quarterly West, Mothering, Dialogue, BYU Studies, Ellipsis, Christian Science Monitor,* and others. She is currently poetry editor for *Sunstone*. She and her husband, Jerry, have raised their family of six children in Richland, Washington, along the Columbia River.

ALLISON PINGREE has a Ph.D. in English, specializing in nineteenth- and twentieth-century American literature and culture, from Harvard University. She currently works as an associate director of the Derek Bok Center for Teaching and Learning at Harvard. Her daughter, Emma Pingree Cannon, was born in September 1993.

LOUISE PLUMMER is a member of the English department faculty at Brigham Young University.

CAROL BENNION QUIST teaches English and humanities at Salt Lake Community College, and is the official manager at *Sunstone* magazine. She has earned prizes and publication for fiction, non-fiction, light verse, and poetry, and currently edits "Poetry Panorama," the semi-annual Utah State Poetry Society publication.

DIAN SADERUP lives with her family in Orem, Utah.

TESSA MEYER SANTIAGO has three children and teaches in the English and honors departments at Brigham Young University.

LINDA SILLITOE is the mother of three children and eight books, including *Crazy for Living: Poems, Sideways to the Sun*, and *Secrets Keep*, all published by Signature Books, as well as five non-fiction works. She currently lives and works in the Phoenix area.

As the daughter of an Air Force pediatrician, HEIDI HEMMING SMITH seems to have sand in her shoes despite a conflicting language for a permanent place to call home. After serving an LDS mission in Ireland, she married her friend and fellow theatre buff Zeric, and upon completion of their bachelor's degrees they spent two and a half years in West Africa with the Peace Corps. The mother of two memorable children, Colin and Copeland, Heidi currently resides in Columbia, South Carolina. An elementary school teacher, she spends much of her life nurturing small things, including people, plants, and animals. She also enjoys trying exotic recipes and is a sometime artist and photographer.

STEPHANIE SMITH-WATERMAN is an education researcher for a Boston consulting firm. She lives in Cambridge, Massachusetts, with her husband, Bryan Waterman, and their two daughters, Anna and Molly.

JAN STUCKI lives in Salt Lake City. She is the mother of two daughters.

JULIE TURLEY lives and writes in New York City.

HOLLY WELKER grew up in southern Arizona and served an LDS mission in Taiwan. She has a B.A. and an M.F.A. from the University of Arizona and is currently pursuing an M.F.A. in creative non-fiction and a Ph.D. in twentieth-century American literature at the University of Iowa. She has published poetry, fiction, and non-fiction in *Alligator Juniper, Black Warrior Review, Cumberland Poetry Review*,

Dialogue: A Journal of Mormon Thought, Hayden's Ferry Review, Other Voices, Sunstone, and *TriQuarterly.* Her main project at Iowa is a book-length memoir about her mission, tentatively entitled *The Rib Cage.*

MARGARET YOUNG is the author of two short story collections and three novels, including *Dear Stone,* forthcoming.